What They Never Told Me When I Became A

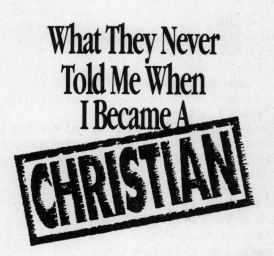

Campus Life Books

After You Graduate
Against All Odds: True Stories of People
　Who Never Gave Up
Alive: Daily Devotions
Alive 2: Daily Devotions
At the Breaking Point: How God Helps Us Through Crisis
The Campus Life Guide to Dating
The Campus Life Guide to Making and Keeping Friends
The Campus Life Guide to Surviving High School
Do You Sometimes Feel Like a Nobody?
Going the Distance: How to Build Your Faith
　for the Long Haul
Life at McPherson High
The Life of the Party: A True Story
　of Teenage Alcoholism
The Lighter Side of Campus Life
Love, Sex & the Whole Person: Everything You Want to
　Know
A Love Story: Questions and Answers on Sex
Making Life Make Sense
Next Time I Fall in Love
Next Time I Fall in Love Journal
Peer Pressure: Making It Work for You
Personal Best: A Campus Life Guide to Knowing
　and Liking Yourself
Welcome to High School
What Teenagers Are Saying about Drugs and Alcohol
What They Never Told Me When I Became a Christian
Worth the Wait: Love, Sex, and Keeping the Dream Alive
You Call This a Family? Making Yours Better

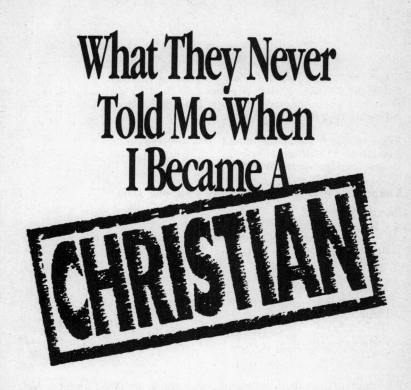

What They Never Told Me When I Became A CHRISTIAN

Verne Becker, Tim Stafford & Philip Yancey

A DIVISION OF CTi
CampusLife BOOKS

ZondervanPublishingHouse
Grand Rapids, Michigan
A Division of HarperCollinsPublishers

What They Never Told Me When I Became a Christian
Copyright © 1986, 1991 by *Campus Life Books*, a division of CTi
Previously published under the title *Questions? Answers!*
All rights reserved

Requests for information should be addressed to:
Zondervan Publishing House
Grand Rapids, Michigan 49530

Library of Congress Cataloging-in-Publication Data

Becker, Verne.
   [Questions? Answers!]
   What they never told me when I became a Christian / by Verne
Becker, Tim Stafford, and Philip Yancey.
     p. cm.
   Previously published as: Questions? Answers!
   ISBN 0-310-71171-1
   1. Teenagers—Religious life. I. Stafford, Tim. II. Yancey,
Philip. III. Title.
BV4531.2.B44   1991
248.8'3—dc20
                           91–3488
                             CIP
                             AC

Designed by Rachel Hostetter
Cover design by The Church Art Works

Printed in the United States of America

95 96 97 98 99 00 01 02 /DH/ 11 12 10 9 8 7 6 5 4 3

CONTENTS

INTRODUCTION

Perhaps you remember when you first believed in God. Maybe there was a time when the Bible suddenly seemed to make sense. Or you knew that, without Jesus, life would ultimately disappoint you.

You became a Christian, full of joy, encouragement, and expectation. Finally, life made sense.

Then you faced some great hardship. You prayed, but God seemed distant and disinterested. Your request was ignored.

Or you opened your Bible and found it dry and dull.

Or doubts began to creep into your mind: If there is a loving and powerful God, why is there also suffering? How can I keep believing in a God I cannot see?

Questions pestered you: If I am a forgiven Christian, why do I still feel so guilty? Why is temptation so hard to resist? Why don't I *feel* like a Christian? Why are there so many hypocrites in the church?

What They Never Told Me When I Became a Christian was written out of just such questions and doubts. It is our effort to face the facts honestly, but also to find hopeful answers. Life as a Christian may not be as carefree as some of us once thought, but neither is God as distant as he sometimes seems.

Here's what we have discovered: Our doubts can make us stronger. Our questions can open the door to a deeper understanding of God. Our disappointments can melt away under the love of God.

It is our hope that you will make the same discovery as you read.

MICHAEL SILUK

Fact #1

SOMETIME, SOMEWHERE, YOU WILL SERIOUSLY DOUBT THAT GOD IS REAL

*But So Did Some
Great Believers
in the Bible*

by Verne Becker

It was a Saturday night for lazing around, and that's what I had been doing: listening to records, flipping through magazines, lounging with a friend who had stopped by, snacking on potato chips and Pepsi. I felt relaxed and cheerful.

Then the phone rang. "Hello, Verne?" said a woman's voice. It was Sue, as in Jim and Sue—close friends who had recently moved to Texas.

"Hi, Sue—how's it going?" I said.

"Uh, not very well," she answered. Her voice wavered a bit, and I realized she had a stuffy nose. She didn't sound well at all. My mind flashed through a list of possible problems. *Maybe she has a bad cold,* I guessed. *Or maybe it's even worse—the whole family has come down with something. Maybe something's wrong with their new baby.*

"Jim was in a car accident . . ." Sue said slowly. *Oh no!* I thought during the half-second before her next words. *What a terrible thing to happen! Here they are trying to get adjusted to all the changes a baby brings, and now Jim cracks up the car and gets stuck in the hospital. No wonder Sue's so upset—*

"... and he's dead, Verne! Jim's dead!" she blurted out, dissolving into tears.

"WHAT?" I gasped. "NO!"

Numbed with shock and disbelief, I spent the remainder of the evening stumbling around the house, alternately flopping on the bed, curling up on the sofa, sitting in silence at the kitchen table, trying to take it all in.

I had known Jim for ten years. We had gone through a lot together as college roommates, as co-workers on the newspaper staff, as guys falling in and out of love with girls. Even when he married Sue and later moved a thousand miles away, I knew we'd still keep in touch regularly. Only a few weeks ago I had rejoiced with them over Trey's birth. And only three days ago it had been Jim's birthday. But it didn't matter now. Jim was gone. Why?

For the next week, as I witnessed the wake, the funeral, the burial, the grief, I did what I could to comfort Jim's family, his friends, and Sue. But even as I tried to assure them of God's love and care, my own mind was a maze of hazy, jumbled thoughts. What did I know of God's love and care? God had just let my best friend die. Or maybe he even *caused* his death.

Not only did I have difficulty comforting the bereaved family, but I didn't very graciously accept others' attempts to comfort me. I heard a wide variety of pat phrases and explanations, all of which I knew were given with the best motives, but none of which provided answers.

One day, as I was talking with two close friends of Jim, I heard strikingly contrasting responses to his death. One friend—obviously red-eyed with sadness—kept saying things like, "Well, he's with the Lord now ..." and "He's better off than we are ..."

Yes, those things are no doubt true, I thought, *but I don't want to hear them right now. Those statements don't answer my "Why" questions.*

I had hardly completed my thoughts when the other friend interrupted. "Will you shut up?" he retorted. "Don't give me any of that sweetsie stuff!" His eyes, also red, flashed with anger. A chilling silence fell over the three of us.

I wasn't sure just what to think about my friend's angry response. But something about it seemed more human, more real— maybe even more *comforting*—than the syrupy lines oozing from my other friend.

LIFE IS NOT SO SIMPLE

Jim's untimely death caused me to reflect on other events that don't fit tidy explanations. For example, African famine: someone responds by saying, "Well, it's terrible, but if it happened, it must be God's will." (Well, yes, in a sense nothing happens outside of God's will, but does God really want those thousands of people to starve?)

Or upon hearing that a close friend is dying, someone says, "Hey don't worry—all things work together for good." (Maybe they do, but why do things have to start out bad before they end up good? And just what is good about someone— Jim, for instance—dying while still in his twenties?)

"I'm scared that if I question God he will send me to hell."

Or in talking about a kid who's plagued with emotional problems, someone comments, "There must be sin in his life." (Why automatically blame the kid for his problems? Suppose he has irresponsible or even abusive parents. And besides, don't *all* people have sin in their lives?)

Or someone tells a friend who's facing some serious tensions in his family, "Just pray about it. Give it up to the Lord." (Prayer and trust are fine, but what should the person say when his dad yells at him?)

Before Jim's death I hadn't worried about the gap between these phrases and reality. In fact, I had used some of the phrases myself. But nowadays I find myself using them a lot less.

Why? The simple reason is that life isn't as simple as I'd like it to be. I grew up thinking that most of the problems of life could be broken down into a series of questions and answers, like a cosmic game of Trivial Pursuit. Every question had an answer, if I just thought hard enough. But as I've gotten older, more and more unanswerable questions have arisen. Or the simplistic answers I'd previously accepted no longer seemed to satisfy.

The Overflow Factor

Has anything ever happened to you—a death, a disappointment, an unanswered prayer—that caused you to question God? If it has, you already know something of the anguish and confusion that accompany such events. You find yourself asking questions— sticky questions such as, "How can God be good if he allowed this to happen?" "Why didn't God intervene and prevent it?" "If God is in my life, why don't I feel him?" "If premarital sex is wrong, why does God allow it to be such a great temptation?" "If God makes such a difference in our lives, why do I know so many Christians who are hypocrites?"

If you haven't yet faced a faith-rocking situation, be forewarned: The day will come when the normal string of events in your life will unravel. No matter how hard you try, you won't be able to twist the strands back together again. You too will start asking hard questions.

A friend of mine put it this way: We all have a bin in our brain labeled "Questions I Can't Answer." As we grow up, a question arises here and there, we toss it in the bin, and pretty much forget about it. But the older we get, the more questions go into the bin, and the fuller it gets. Eventually the bin overflows, forcing the questions into our conscious thinking, and pushing us to look for answers. The overflow point differs for each person, but each year we live brings us closer to it.

Consider another analogy. Take an uninflated beach ball and try to hold it underwater. Effortless. Now blow it up a little bit and try again. Slightly more difficult. Blow it up further. And further. By the time you fully inflate the beach ball, you'll find it impossible to hold underwater for any length of time.

Think of your questions as the air inside that beach ball. As they add up over time, they become more difficult to hold under. One day they burst to the surface.

This book will give you the chance to tackle some of those questions before they tackle you. It focuses on the issues that typically lead people to doubt God—pain and frustration, conflicting feelings, strong temptations, unanswered prayers, hypocrisy and legalism. Each chapter zeroes in on one issue and offers answers that I hope will reduce your internal confusion.

PORTRAIT OF A DOUBTER

Is doubt wrong? Does it cause you to lose your faith? How you feel about doubts and questions probably depends on your family and church background. The more strictly your parents protect their values and beliefs, the less freedom you've probably felt to call those beliefs into question. In some families and churches, doubters feel guilty or ashamed.

When people doubt, they're sometimes viewed as having a "problem." Perhaps you've heard someone who was asking questions described as "rebellious," "backsliding," or "immature."

Of course, not all doubters are serious about their doubts. Often they're not really interested in answers. They may use their questions as a smoke screen to avoid facing the truth about themselves. Others may say they doubt, when in reality they don't question the truth of Christianity at all; they simply aren't willing to *obey* the truth they already know.

But there is such a thing as true doubting—the kind of doubting that ultimately can lead to greater understanding, deeper faith, and a closer relationship to God. True doubters are special people, people not satisfied with simplistic answers to complicated questions. Though their doubts often trouble them, they take time to think, to read, to talk with others in search of understanding. They are people dedicated to truth.

When you first decided to follow Jesus you were asking questions like, "How can I make sense of life?" "How can I tell right from wrong?" "What happens after I die?" "How do I deal with guilt?" You probably found answers to those questions. Straightforward, satisfying answers to these and a host of other questions can be found in the pages of the Bible. It informs you that God created you, and it gives your life meaning as you seek his will. It offers guidelines to live by. When you sin, the Bible tells you that God forgives you because his Son, Jesus Christ, took the punishment in your place when he died on the cross. It tells you death is not the end, but rather the beginning of forever-life with God.

Nothing should ever hide the basic importance of those answers. But as you progress in your Christian life, new questions will arise—the kind of questions the Bible doesn't give complete answers to. These are the questions you'll explore further in this book.

In Good Company

If you ever worry that you're the only one who's ever doubted God, look a little closer at the Bible. You may expect to find saint after saint proclaiming victory over doubts. On the contrary, many people in the Bible stumbled over hard questions. And I don't mean insignificant characters buried in long lists of genealogies. I'm talking about big names.

Job in the Old Testament garnered fame for his pointed questions to God about suffering. Listen to some of them: "Why is a man allowed to be born if God is only going to give him a hopeless life of uselessness and frustration?" (Job 3:23 LB). "O God, am I some monster, that you never let me alone? Even when I try to forget my misery in sleep, you terrify with nightmares . . . What is

mere man that you should spend your time persecuting him?"
(7:12–14, 17 LB). "Does it really seem right to you to oppress and
despise me, a man you have made; and to send joy and prosperity to
the wicked?" (10:3 LB). Not exactly simple questions. But God
never condemned Job for asking them.

David, the shepherd-king of Israel, questioned God on numer-
ous occasions. In his psalms, he poured out his feelings to God
regardless of whether they were joyful, sorrowful, fearful or
doubtful. In Psalm 22 he wrote, "Why are you so far from saving
me, so far from the words of my groaning? O my God, I cry out by
day, but you do not answer, by night, and am not silent" (vv. 1, 2).
Or in Psalm 13: "How long, O LORD? Will you forget me forever?
How long will you hide your face from me? How long must I wrestle
with my thoughts and every day have sorrow in my heart? How long
will my enemy triumph over me?" (vv. 1, 2). Yet God still remained
faithful to David in spite of his questions.

Or read these depressing words, often attributed to Solomon:
"Everything is meaningless. . . . What a heavy burden God has laid
on men! I have seen all the things that are done under the sun; all of
them are meaningless, a chasing after the wind" (Ecclesiastes 1:2,
13, 14).

In the New Testament, doubters also appear. John the Baptist
had met Jesus personally and baptized him, yet he later wondered
whether Jesus was indeed the Messiah (Matthew 11:2–6; Luke
7:18–23). Jesus didn't criticize John, but told him to look at the
evidence and not lose faith. Even Jesus expressed uncertainty about
God's plan for the world. In the Garden of Gethsemane, Jesus
prayed, in effect, "God, isn't there some other way to do this? Do I
really have to die?" And on the cross, Jesus also cried out in
anguish, with perhaps the most haunting words in all of Scripture,
"My God, my God, why have you forsaken me?" (Mark 15:34,
originally stated in Psalm 22:1).

Last but not least is Doubting Thomas, perhaps the most
notorious questioner in the Bible (John 20:24–29). He boldly
declared that he wouldn't believe that Jesus had really risen from the
dead unless he could see Jesus for himself and even touch his

wounds. When Thomas finally saw Jesus, what did Jesus tell him? "OK, Thomas, do it. Touch me. Now stop doubting and believe." But he went on to say, "Thomas, you've got it easy because you can see me. Greater blessings will go to those who *haven't* seen me and still believe." Jesus did not condemn Thomas for doubting. Instead, he answered Thomas's doubt and warned him that others in the future would find faith even more difficult.

Surely, if all these biblical people could express doubts to God without being condemned, it must be OK for you to do the same. The Bible indicates that God welcomes doubters and questioners. Try to keep this in mind as you read through the rest of the book. God gives you the freedom to doubt, to look for answers, to seek the truth. (After all, he *is* Truth.) So give yourself that same freedom. If you diligently seek the truth, you will find it.

MICHAEL SILUK

Fact #2

YOU WON'T ALWAYS FEEL GREAT ABOUT BEING A CHRISTIAN

But Your Relationship to God Goes Deeper Than Feelings

by Verne Becker

Doubts can arise for many reasons. Maybe you doubt because you're still wrestling with the Big Questions—tragedy and suffering, unanswered prayer, the problem of evil, etc. We'll be dealing with some of these questions in the chapters that follow.

But perhaps your doubts are like Becky's. A new Christian, she questioned her faith while working a summer job as a forest ranger. And her questioning centered not on the Big Questions, but mainly on her feelings. Here's how she explained it.

It was my third summer in the mountains of Colorado; I was the veteran, all-pro ranger. That's why I couldn't let anybody see what I was about to do.

Glancing around me, I tiptoed past Peggy's cassette player and knelt down on the drab brown Forest Service carpet. I felt pretentious, so I sat back on my heels and stared at my hands folded in my lap.

"OK, uh . . . God, I believe in you—I mean I accept you . . . that is, I accept Jesus . . . and . . . I'm asking

*Jesus into my heart." I blurted out these words I'd heard
Christians use and I waited. I listened. Nothing. I didn't
expect bells, but I was sure there was supposed to be
something—a supernatural shiver, at least. Something! But
I felt disgustingly unchanged.*

What did I do wrong? I wondered.

*I squeezed my eyes shut and wrinkled my face, I
couldn't even work up a warm glow. All I felt was my
feet going to sleep—and I knew that was from the ridicu-
lous posture, not from some heavy spiritual transformation.
And I still smelled Friday night's pork and beans—I
knew that people who had just been born again would not
smell pork and beans.*

*Leaning on the orange crate under the cassette player, I
slowly rose onto my tingling feet.*

"Maybe the time's just not right, huh God?"

*I limped to my room, even though it was only 8:30
P.M., and slumped onto my squeaky army cot.*

*There was just something about those Christians I'd run
across—they seemed confident and secure in a way I
wasn't. I was sick of all my insecurities, and I'd finally
decided I wanted whatever it was they had.*

*Now, I was sure I had blown it. Apparently my fum-
bled prayer to God hadn't scored a direct hit. I did not
feel transformed. I felt sleepy, just as I had the night
before. Wondering why I'd been born the first time, I fell
asleep.*

Later Becky ran into a Christian family at the campground and
had a chance to ask them some questions.

"So, you've come to the Lord?" Bob said.

*"Yeah," I answered. "I came, but I don't think it
took! Nothing happened. It wasn't an experience, you*

know, like I've heard about. Like people falling over or throwing down their crutches. I felt nothing, except three minutes older. I don't know if I'm saved or just shelved for a while."

Becky doubted because she didn't *feel* the way she thought a Christian should feel. For some reason, her feelings didn't rally to her support when she committed her life to God.

Did the same thing happen to you when you first became a Christian? Or have you experienced other times when your feelings don't agree with your beliefs? For example: You ask God to forgive you for a sin, knowing that the Bible says he will (1 John 1:9), but you still feel guilty afterwards.

Or you find you can't keep your mind on the Bible, no matter how strongly you believe it to be God's Word.

Or you try to maintain a loving attitude toward someone who has wronged you, but anger seems to get in the way.

Or you sit in a church pew Sunday morning but don't feel particularly worshipful—whatever "worshipful" is.

Or you hear people tell you they feel a "peace" about a decision they've made, but, try as you will, you feel nothing but confusion about yours.

Just what do feelings have to do with your faith? Is it even *possible* to feel God? Why do your feelings sometimes conflict with what you believe? Before we answer these questions, let's take a closer look at the nature of feelings.

Natural and Normal

Feelings are the emotional/physical reactions we experience in everyday living, mostly in the context of relationships. Someone tells you how nice you look in a new outfit, and you feel good. Your boyfriend shows up late for a date, and you feel angry. You lie to your parents after missing curfew, and you feel guilty. A test is coming up, and you feel anxiety. You score the lowest grade, and you feel ashamed.

Feelings give you information that helps you relate to other people, understand yourself and your needs, and make decisions. They are natural, normal, and good. Feelings aren't right or wrong in themselves; they're just there. Your job is to be aware of them and learn to interpret what they are telling you. They don't make any decisions for you; you have to decide how to act upon them. It's the actions, not the feelings, that can be right or wrong.

The funny thing about feelings is that they can be both reliable and unreliable at the same time. In one sense, a feeling is *always* true: If you're angry that your girlfriend is late, even a legitimate excuse from her does not change the fact that you feel angry. Once you hear her excuse, you may feel differently. But whether she meant to or not, your girlfriend hurt your feelings; a good relationship depends on working that hurt out. The feeling is a true description of what happened between you.

> **"I wonder why I don't have the peace and joy that come with being a Christian. Why am I so lonely and depressed?"**

On the other hand, feelings can be unreliable as prescriptions for action. Just because you *feel* excited about taking a Florida vacation with several school friends doesn't mean you *should* go—particularly if you have to skip two final exams in the process.

Feelings always provide accurate information about yourself, but not necessarily accurate recommendations for action. It's often great to act on your urge to hug someone, but not so great to act on your desire to punch someone out. Whether the action is right or wrong, however, the feeling is still real.

Many of the struggles you face boil down to a conflict between what you feel you'd like to do and what you believe you should do.

You either act too quickly on your feelings or divorce yourself from them completely. You either break dishes or fake a sweet smile. Neither response is healthy. One of the biggest challenges of life is to balance feelings and principles without minimizing the importance of either.

When someone offends you, the healthy response begins with listening to your feeling and identifying it. (Anger? Hurt? etc.) Then try to pinpoint first the immediate and then the underlying causes of your feeling. (Example: "When he said I stink at basketball, I felt angry. But I know I'm not the greatest in that sport, and I've frequently felt inferior to the other guys I play with. What he said triggered my frustration in sports.")

When you've done that, you'll find you're in a better position to decide what to *do* with your feeling. You may choose to talk to the person. You may decide to practice your jump-shot. You may realize the most important thing is that you take time to understand you feelings before acting on them. That's how you learn and grow as a person.

WHERE DOES FAITH FIT?

Now that we've taken a brief look at the nature of feelings, how does faith fit into the picture? Your feelings about God are really not so different from your feelings toward other people.

It's perfectly normal to expect your feelings about God to be great. With all the wonderful promises in the Bible about God's love and his care, you naturally expect to feel constantly delighted with him. Maybe you did when you first became a Christian. However, few, if any, people find that their feelings about God stay on a constant high. They experience low points.

You can exhibit two extremes in handling your feelings about God: acting them out automatically, or denying them altogether. For the first extreme, you might say, "I don't feel God's presence when I pray, so he must not be there." So you quit praying. Or, like

Becky, you say, "I just haven't felt any different since I committed my life to Jesus, so he must not be real."

For the opposite extreme, you might smile your way through life, simply reciting a Bible verse as a Band-Aid to any perplexing situation.

The most healthy approach is to find a balance between your feelings and faith. When you don't feel the way you think you should, don't conclude that your beliefs are all wrong. But don't deny or disregard your doubts and questions either. Listen closely to them. Try to understand and accept them. And as you search for the underlying sources of those feelings, they will teach you about yourself—your needs, your longings, your hurts, and how these affect your relationship to God.

You and Your Worldview

Most people, when they feel disappointed with God, look for something wrong with their relationship to God. They either assume they are unforgivable sinners—and so God can't give them the blessings he promises—or else they assume that all those promises of the Bible were really deceptive advertising.

In reality, such bad feelings often don't come from God at all. Bad feelings usually come straight from your past, which has given you certain assumptions about how the world, including God, ought to behave. These influences will be the major factors in your feelings toward God.

Alvin Toffler, author of *Future Shock* and *The Third Wave*, describes a worldview as a "mental model of the world," and compares it to a giant filing cabinet in your brain. As you grow up, the situations and people you encounter provide you with information that you file away in your mind—information about God, about human nature, about good and evil, about the purpose of life.

"A worldview, in other words, is a map of reality," writes James Sire in *The Joy of Reading*. "Like any map, it may fit what is really there or it may be grossly misleading. The map is not the world itself, of course, only an image of it, more or less accurate in some places, distorted in others. Still all of us carry around such a map in our mental makeup, and we act on it. All of our thinking presupposes it. Most of our experience fits into it."

For instance, the culture you live in influences your worldview. Iranians grow up with a different concept of God than Americans. Citizens of the Soviet Union, an officially atheistic state, are inclined not to believe in a personal yet all-powerful God. Here in the U.S., particularly in the past few years, the idea of a personal God has gained very wide acceptance.

Even the area of the country you live in can affect your outlook. There's the conservative Bible Belt, the liberal Northeast, and the free 'n' easy West Coast, all of which promote their own styles of faith and worldview. City dwellers may look at the world differently than suburban or rural types.

> **"I'm always in a bad mood. I worry about everything and can't stop letting things get to me."**

Financial status can also play a part. Wealth may cause you to believe you need many more things than you actually do. It can create an artificial sense of power and independence, tempting you to think you can get along without God. Poverty may cause you to thank God for a mere bowl of rice for dinner, but it may also produce in you a hopeless, pessimistic approach to life.

The religious subculture you live in can profoundly affect your worldview. A Presbyterian's outlook on life will differ from a Pentecostal's. A Catholic, Episcopalian, or other liturgical church setting may threaten and alienate you if you attended First Baptist throughout your childhood.

There are still other factors, such as the temperament you were born with, the friends you hang around with, and the tragedies or other crises you've experienced. All of these factors contribute to the person you are and the way you view the world.

Doubts begin when you encounter something that doesn't fit with your mental map. A close friend dies suddenly; your parents divorce; the Christian you most respected gives up the faith; the college you had your heart set on attending rejects you; you don't feel the way you think a Christian ought to. You must then decide whether you want to revise your worldview to allow for this new information.

Sometimes your feelings may lead you to change your beliefs. Some of what you believe about God may represent an incomplete or twisted view of what God says about himself in the Bible. In such a case, your feelings can lead you to a deeper knowledge of the true God.

Just as often, though, your core beliefs about God aren't wrong. You just see them through your past—and your past makes you react to God in a particular way.

The Family Effect

Probably the strongest influence on your worldview is your family. The thickest files in your mental cabinet contain information about the way your parents treated you as a child.

"When we are children our parents are godlike figures to our child's eye," Christian psychiatrist M. Scott Peck writes. "And the way they do things seems the way they must be done throughout the universe. Our first (and, sadly, often our only) notion of God's nature is a simple extrapolation of our parents' natures, a simple blending of the characters of our mothers and fathers or their substitutes. If we have loving, forgiving parents, we are likely to believe in a loving and forgiving God. And in our adult view, the world is likely to seem as nurturing a place as our childhood was. If our parents are harsh and punitive, we are likely to mature with a concept of a harsh and punitive monster-god. And if they failed to care for us, we will likely envision the universe as similarly uncaring."

In short, we tend to project the feelings we have toward our parents onto God. How did your parents treat you as a child? What kind of worldview do you think their upbringing fostered in you? As you search your past, you may uncover a good explanation for your present feelings toward God. (Keep in mind that what you parents *told* you affects you far less than what they actually *did*.)

For example, if your parents hold you to unrealistically high standards of performance in school, sports, or church, you may struggle to believe that God accepts you as you are, regardless of your performance. Or if your parents pampered you as a child, always giving you whatever you wanted, you may find that you expect the same kind of pampering from God.

Beware of falling into the blame-your-parents trap. Rather than blaming your parents, which is useless, learn from them. You'll need more than an hour, or an afternoon, or even a week to reflect on your family. Some people need years to get a handle on the dynamics of their family and their worldview.

But it is worth the time. Not only will you understand that your feelings about God don't necessarily stem from God, but you will find that with deeper understanding your feelings can change.

FAITH AND FEELINGS IN HARMONY

This process of personalizing your faith doesn't guarantee that you'll never have conflicting feelings about God. No one knows himself or God so thoroughly that he can feel a constant oneness and vitality with God. You'll still feel like you're praying into the air at times. You may still feel guilty even though you "know" God has forgiven you. You may feel just plain lonely and wonder why God isn't taking the loneliness away. But if you take the time to explore your feelings, your faith, and your past, you'll be more likely to *feel* what you believe.

A relationship with God is in many ways like a relationship with a friend or lover. Good feelings take time to develop and deepen. Misunderstandings occur. You're not always on the same wavelength. But in time, you grow to know and understand each other. The difference, of course, is that God doesn't flub up in relationships. Regardless of how you feel about him, he always stays the same. He doesn't grow weary with your doubts. He already knows you and your feelings totally and loves you perfectly, regardless of how you feel.

Even if you've been a Christian for several years, your relationship with God is quite new, especially since it will last forever. So give yourself and God plenty of time to grow closer.

That's the lesson Becky learned as she talked to her friend Bob at the campsite.

"Feelings can be fantastic," Bob said to me, "Fortunately, however, we don't have to have an emotional high to know God. You may not know him well yet, Becky, but he knows you. And whether you realize it or not, he's already at work in your life."

After talking to Bob, I felt so happy I could hardly believe I was only eight thousand feet high. But that night in the Colorado Rockies, I learned that high doesn't matter. I now know when I feel nothing, even when I feel like a forgotten pair of dirty socks, I've still got the most exciting thing in the universe living inside me. A warm glow is nice, but it doesn't bring me any closer to God. Jesus is at home in a cool heart just as he is in a warm one.

MICHAEL SILUK

Fact #3

SOMETIMES TEMPTATION WILL SEEM TOO TOUGH TO RESIST

But You Can Overcome It

Tim Stafford

Feelings, as we've seen, don't necessarily reflect reality. You can feel that God is far away, for instance, when in fact he is immediately available to you.

Sometimes, though, you feel far from God for what seems to be a very realistic reason. Do you know what I find more discouraging than anything else in my life as a Christian? It's the feeling I get right after I have given in, again, to temptation—after I look at a dirty magazine, for instance.

Temptation is so pervasive, so personal. Doesn't God understand that we humans cannot simply flip an internal switch and automatically say no to everything? I find myself failing again and again and again.

So I have thought about temptation, wondering why God allows it, and whether there is a magic secret to resisting it. "Yielding to God" or "turning to the Lord" are phrases that have helped me at times. But I have found there is no magic in phrases. I cannot turn away from temptation just by putting myself through some mental gymnastics.

Such religious "techniques" have sometimes left me very

discouraged. They make me think I have the answer. Then, giving in to temptation again, I abruptly know that I don't. And my doubts return.

TAKING A CLOSER LOOK

It has helped, though, to think through the nature of temptation. Is there some consistent trend I can discern in it? I have found three different components to temptation.

Temptation Can Be a Physical Object You Encounter

Temptation is a beautiful woman you can easily turn into an object instead of a person by letting her body preoccupy your thoughts.

Temptation is a piece of pie when you are trying to lose weight.

Temptation is a pornographic magazine.

Temptation is too much change returned by a cashier.

If you want to avoid temptation, avoid these objects as much as you possibly can. Unfortunately, some of those objects are not easy to stay away from without becoming a hermit.

Temptation Is a Pressured Situation

Temptation is when everyone kids you and eggs you to do something you would rather not.

Temptation is when your boss jumps on your back, and you feel like lashing out at him or her.

Temptation is when you are in a group of strangers who are laughing and have a good time among themselves, and you feel like creeping away and feeling sorry for yourself.

By yourself you might not want to do the things those situations tempt you to do. You wouldn't gossip if you weren't around friends who were gossiping. You wouldn't swear if your friends didn't. In certain situations, however, you find yourself doing what you otherwise would not.

Some of those situations you can stay away from, just as you can stay away from tempting objects. If a group of your friends is constantly in trouble, you may need to find new friends. Or you may need to keep away from them when they're out for trouble.

Other situations you may be able to defuse. One well-placed remark may loosen up a tense moment. You can become a leader in your group instead of a follower. You can sit down with your boss and explain how you feel so that he or she won't be so prone to jump on you.

Unfortunately, some pressure situations are not easy to avoid or change. Temptation seems inevitable.

Temptation Is a Voice in Your Head Trying to Deceive You

Temptation says, "You're worthless. Why try?"

Temptation says, "If they treat you like that, you ought to treat them the same way. They deserve it."

Temptation says, "What difference does it make if you do it one more time?"

Temptation works from inside, calling into question what God says is true and scattering half-truths inside your mind. This is the most devastating aspect of temptation. Tempting objects and pressuring situations are not enough. They must be accompanied by an invasion of your brain. Obviously you can't run from your own thoughts. You can be tempted anywhere, anytime—in church, alone, in the wilderness (where, in fact, Jesus was most severely tempted). So how are you going to "avoid temptation"?

You can't, really. Some people try to lock temptation out of their lives. They go only to "safe" parties and "safe" movies, and they have "safe" friends. They stay away from the beach and from non-Christian books, they build up a set of rules for themselves to follow rigidly so that temptation will never find a crack in their personalities. All these actions may be appropriate at times. But any real solution has to deal with the brain as well. If you are free from temptation in your own thoughts, you can conquer the problems friends and things bring into your life.

A HELPFUL ANALOGY

The pressure of temptation is a lot like real, physical pressure. You can "escape" it only to a point. Do you think a submarine, since it's watertight, can go down as deep as it likes? It can't. Even the nuclear submarines built strongly enough to batter through the ice at the North Pole have a maximum depth. A submarine known as *Thresher* exceeded that depth some years ago. When the pressure became too great, the sea water crushed the sub's heavy steel bulkheads as if the submarine were a plastic model. Searchers found only little pieces of that huge ship lying on the ocean floor. That is pressure.

What if you want to go deeper than a submarine can go? There are research crafts built especially for that purpose—steel balls lowered into the ocean on a cable. One researcher can just fit inside, shielded by the heavy steel armor. As he descends, he peers out through a thick glass plate, searching the ocean depths for whatever life may survive under such pressure.

"At school, so many things that I know are wrong look so good, and sometimes I give in. I ask God's forgiveness, but my situation doesn't seem to improve ... what's wrong with me?"

And what does he see? Fish. You might expect these fish, living under such pressure, to be built along the lines of an army tank.

They are not. Where the little submarine has inches of steel to protect it, these fish have normal skin, a fraction of an inch thick. They swim freely and curiously about the craft. They sometimes flash neon lights. They have huge eyes. They are as exotic as any fish in the ocean.

How can they survive so freely under such pressure? They have a secret: equal and opposite pressure inside themselves.

In real life, some Christians deal with pressure by putting on inches of steel plate. They shield themselves from the outside world and strap themselves into a narrow space, peering out into the darkness. They are safe inside. But God's kind of freedom is more like the fish's. We keep our shape, not through steel plate, but by God's Spirit, who gives us inside strength to deal with each pressure point in our lives.

Romans 12:2, a noted passage of the Bible, essentially says this: "Don't be squeezed into the mold of this world, but be transformed by the renewing of your mind." Pressure from the outside acts to make you conform—to be just like everyone else. The Spirit of God counteracts that from the inside, through your mind.

It's no use pretending temptation doesn't exist. If you are on a diet, a piece of blueberry pie looks appealing, and there is nothing evil about that. I have heard people say that sin is really no fun, but that is not true. Sin is fun . . . for a while.

What makes sin not fun in the long run are the things that come with it. You may enjoy a piece of pie today, but that means tomorrow you won't enjoy standing on the scales. You may enjoy self-pity today, but if you keep it up, self-pity will become *all* you get to enjoy; you won't have any friends.

Beating Temptation

To change your mind to have the inner strength to push back temptation, you need to appeal to higher loyalties, stronger desires. If you think of it, resisting temptation is basically simple. It's a choice. You can look over the options and decide what you want to do. The problem is that temptation's pleasures are often more obvious and immediate than the pleasures of not giving in. Besides, your mind has been twisted so you cannot always see clearly what is really good for you. It *does* seem better to be loved by your crowd of friends than to be loved by God. So you need to renew you mind— get in touch with what's really best for you. You need to retrain your thinking so that those rewards become as obvious as the rewards you get for giving in to temptation. Perhaps these principles will help that process.

1. *Know what you're getting into.* Think about the long-term results of how you act. Today it may be easier to fight with your parents and get your own way. But what kind of relationship are you building for the future? On the other hand, what will obeying God lead to? If you can see the attraction of the life God wants to plant in you, you will be less tempted to choose some other, short-term pleasure.

The Bible is full of commentary on how good a godly life is. Many of the psalms speak of the sheer enjoyment of being in touch with God, obedient to him, relishing the joys of his world. Some of the psalms also frankly confront the doubts and bitter feelings that come when you see unbelievers happy and successful without God, while your godliness seems unrewarded. Read those psalms (for instance, Psalms 37, 49, and 73) and work on appreciating the advantages of not giving in to temptation. Do it daily.

2. *Replace tempting thoughts with something better.* You can't ignore temptation, but you can fill your thoughts with other things. Often prayer helps—and not necessarily prayer for help in resisting temptation. I often begin praying for friends. Sometimes, too, when you are feeling tempted it is very helpful to remind yourself of the power and love of Jesus, who is on your side, who lives with you. Some people use this verse "I can do everything through him who gives me strength" (Philippians 4:13).

You don't have to fill your mind with religious thoughts. Sometimes the best thing you can do is to pick up an interesting book, call up a friend, or start working on a project. If you are tempted to go to an X-rated movie, look for another movie instead.

The problem with many temptations is that they are close and immediate. If you can put them off a while and give your mind a chance to recover from its panic, you will be in better shape to see the bigger picture.

3. *Your mind tends to follow patterns. Change patterns, and you change your mind.* In some families, kids are always fighting over what TV programs to watch. They should change the pattern by figuring out ahead of time what shows they will watch and reach some compromise long before the tube is turned on.

For me, being tired often means getting depressed. I can lecture myself that I have no right to feel so sorry for myself. But a more effective solution is to go to bed when I am tired. Somehow that takes the drama out of resisting temptation. I outflank it instead of pacing the floor and praying for strength to resist it.

Breaking habits often requires persistent hard work. You must first find out what starts you into the pattern leading to failure. Then, you must break the pattern in its beginning stages. No matter how innocent those early stages may seem, you must be merciless with them. People seldom break a bad pattern overnight. Gradually, painfully, they fight their way out of it.

4. *Break the pattern of failure by confession.* When you go over your mistakes with another person, it changes your attitude. For one thing, you receive forgiveness, and your mind is put at rest. You don't get down on yourself and repeat your failures because of an "I-did-it-once-what-does-one-more-time-matter?" attitude. For another thing, a friend can help strengthen you. He or she can check up on you, encourage you, and pray for you. He or she can remind you of God's limitless forgiveness.

"I struggle because some things that aren't pleasing to God are fun, and sometimes I'm not really sure what is right or wrong."

God's Limitless Forgiveness

As you try to identify and break bad patterns, remember that everyone has at least one area of special weakness. There you may find temptation too strong. You may become discouraged and doubtful of God's goodness.

At these times you must remember the limitless nature of God's forgiveness. It is limitless, which is hard for us to grasp. But if you cling to it, you will be lifted out of your discouragement. Not only that, but the area you are weakest in can be transformed into special strength.

5. *Above all, remember who you are: a child of God, loved by him.* When tempting thoughts come, recall that fact to your mind: "I could act that way, but does that really bring honor to God? Because of the way he treats me, I want to be loyal and loving to him."

The more you understand God's love, the more you will want to be close to him and obedient to him. As you grow in Christ, some of your temptations will simply vanish—they will begin to seem stupid. Their pleasures will be insignificant compared with the good things you are experiencing.

Many people have found that studying Scripture, and even memorizing certain verses, can be a great help in resisting temptation. Not that it's magic, quoting Scripture to make the problems go away. Scripture simply reminds you of the voice of God himself and of his desires for your life. Jesus, when tempted by Satan, referred back to the book of Deuteronomy and found his guidance there. You can too—so long as you know Scripture well enough to be able to use it under pressure.

Reinforce your understanding of your true identity not only by reading the Bible and applying what it says, but also by talking to God, by talking with Christian friends, by listening to what pastors and other Christians say, and especially by worshiping and thanking God for what he has done for you. The disciplined habit of going to church and fellowshiping with other Christians is a powerful force in shaping your sense of being in Christ's family. Christ's message to you is this: You simply don't have to act in the old way. You are a new person with a whole new way of acting. Jesus will help you live up to your new self.

You get stronger every time you beat temptation. Each success is an exercise building you up. Perhaps that's part of the reason God permits temptation rather than taking it all away: because temptation gives you a chance to strengthen your spiritual muscles, to focus on the things in life that are most important. When you're under temptation, you can have no doubt about needing God's help. When you resist temptation through God's help, you have no doubt about the direction you have chosen: It's wonderful to work on God's side.

There will always be temptations as long as you live on this earth. And you will always fail God at some point. Both temptation and failure should remind you to rely on God for forgiveness of your sins, for the desire to change your life, and the power to change your life. The closer you come to God, the less you will want to disappoint him. And the less you will doubt his purposes for you.

MICHAEL SILUK

Fact #4

GUILTY FEELINGS DON'T ALWAYS DISAPPEAR WHEN GOD FORGIVES YOU

*But God's View
Matters Much More
Than Yours*

Tim Stafford

Kathy grew up in a church where she got the idea that God watched her like a hawk from heaven, counting up her sins. You could see by the way she walked and the way her eyes never met anyone else's that she was ashamed to be alive.

Then eventually, she came to understand that Jesus was willing to take her just the way she was, to love her and heal her from all guiltiness. For a while she walked around feeling as though she had new running shoes: Everything seemed lighter, happier, and freer.

Strangely, this sensation wore off. Her initial wonder at being accepted and loved grew old. Many of the patterns she had expected God to change hung on. She still did things she knew God didn't like, and she began feeling guilty again.

It did not help that Kathy went to a church where guilt was regularly hammered in. When she read a chapter of the Bible that others found encouraging, she found every word aimed at her failures. A single word about sin was enough to bring a week-long attack of guilt. She was just naturally sensitive, and after the initial relief of forgiveness had worn off, her Christianity seemed to make her guilt greater, not less.

A non-Christian psychologist, concluding that most of her problems were related to her faith, tried to "cure" her of that. He did not believe in such a thing as guilt. He thought the best thing for everyone was to "feel good about yourself." For Kathy, he certainly had a point: guilt paralyzed her. It kept her from serving others. She even began to question whether she really was a Christian.

It was difficult to argue with Kathy about her guilt. To her Christian friends, the sins bothering her didn't seem very great. They certainly had greater problems which didn't paralyze them with guilt. In fact, when they talked to her they felt uncomfortable: Maybe they should feel as guilty as she did! They didn't know how to help Kathy. They could only listen to her while she spilled out her guilty feelings.

AN UNRELIABLE CONSCIENCE

Kathy was an extreme case, but by no means a unique one. Many psychologists would list guilt as one of the chief problems of their disturbed clients. Often it seems to afflict the most religious people. Why does Christianity, which promises to forgive and heal guilt, sometimes seem to bring on more?

The instrument that tells you that you're guilty is usually called the conscience. It communicates through your emotions and warns you when there is a problem in your life.

The conscience is very much like your body's pain-sensing system. When you cut your finger, the dripping blood is an indisputable fact. Anyone can see that it needs attention. But the pain that comes with the cut makes it urgent. This can be very annoying if you are doing something you want to do, like learning a new move on your skateboard. You would rather put off dealing with your cut. But pain won't let you.

Your conscience is designed to respond the same way to sin. If something is wrong in your life, guilty feelings force your attention onto the sore spot, making you drop everything else until you attend to it. It is God's way of making you feel the same way he feels about sin. But one huge problem comes up: Your conscience is unreliable. Sometimes it sends guilt messages which are inaccurate or inappropriate.

Your pain-sensing system is, by contrast, quite reliable. If you feel physical pain there is nearly always a cut to go with it. Yet imaginary pains do exist. Amputees sometimes receive terrible pain from a "phantom limb" that no longer exists.

Such imaginary problems show up much more often with your conscience. One person feels guilty about premarital sex, and another doesn't. One person feels guilty because he stole from K-Mart, and another doesn't. One person feels guilty for going to a dance, while another wouldn't even think about it. The explanation is simple: God made your pain-sensing system, but your conscience is largely man-made. We tend to think that our conscience is the voice of God, but it is really more the voice of our parents and our society, plus our experience, formed over many years. If you were raised poorly, or spent years turning off your conscience's warnings, your conscience may be far out of register.

In other words, real guilt is not the same as guilt feelings. People like Kathy are mostly plagued with false, not real, guilt. They have an oversensitive conscience which isn't tuned into the reality of God's teaching in the Bible. Someone needs to ask Kathy, "Is this real guilt or false?" Often people who have a bad self-image use false or imagined guilt to punish themselves.

Distinguishing False Guilt from True

A sign of false guilt is that you can't pin it down. False guilt often arises in response to persistent mental fantasies, to feelings and temptations. It seldom stems from a specific action that can be changed. If it does, the action is frequently morally arguable—such as masturbation or dancing—or something done long in the past. I have noticed that chronically guilty people seldom agonize over something the Bible indisputably condemns. They worry about the gray areas.

This leads me to think that false guilt is often a temptation sent by Satan, meant to divert our attention from God's wonderful forgiveness and from real problems that God wants to change. False guilt needs to be faced for exactly what it is. If you experience false guilt, don't pray to God (for the hundredth time) to forgive it. Instead, ask him to help you leave such self-hating feelings behind and get on with life.

"When I do something wrong and then pray for God's forgiveness again and again, I worry that he might be discouraged with me because I can't keep in line and do his will."

In fact, this is just what 1 John 3:18–20 suggests: "Our love should not be just words and talk; it must be true love, which shows itself in action. This, then, is how we will know that we belong to the truth. This is how our hearts will be confident in God's presence. *If our heart condemns us, we know that God is greater than our heart, and that he knows everything"* (TEV).

Rather than being paralyzed by guilt, we are to get on with obeying God through active love. Nothing can better reassure us of God's real love.

You can tune your conscience to reality—though it takes time—by confronting false guilt, and by trying to absorb God's biblical standards of right and wrong. A bad conscience is man-made—and so is a good one. If you surround yourself with people who reinforce God's standards and challenge your "false guilt," you will gradually begin to think as they do.

A good, accurate conscience is basically a shortcut. It helps you know what you ought to do without having to ponder your action. In a sense a conscience is an automatic pilot. Your conscience will guide you through millions of choices each day without a thought. You don't have to think about whether to pay for the shirt you pick up at a department store. You don't have to ponder whether to accept what your father said about getting in on time. You don't have to wonder whether to cheat each time you take a test. Your conscience saves you the trouble. It lets you concentrate on more difficult choices.

But your conscience is not an infallible guide. It is not the voice of God. It is an emotional response that God has built into your brain. It can be, if you tune it properly, a helpful instrument pushing you to do the right thing. Left untuned, however, it can paralyze you or distract you from what is really important in God's sight.

When You're Really Guilty

So far we have been considering what I call false guilt. What if your guilt is real? What do you do then? I can think of three possible responses.

One is to punish yourself. "I must be a terrible person. Oh, how guilty I am! How much God must feel hurt by me!" This is like a person who, on cutting his finger, sits down in the road and begins to yowl, endlessly screaming how much it hurts. Little children do this, but adults should not. It is not a very good way to respond to pain—or to guilt feelings.

Another response is to deny that the guilt exists at all. "Guilt is a neurotic impulse. It cripples and represses many wonderful people and keeps them from enjoying life. God wants me to feel happy. Therefore I will never let myself feel guilty." This is like a person who makes up his mind to totally ignore pain: "Pain is a weakness. Only weak people feel pain. I'm tough, too tough for that." The macho act of ignoring pain turns you into a totally insensitive person. Ignoring guilt will also make you insensitive, and you will usually end up inflicting much more real guilt on yourself, whether you feel that guilt or not. In our time, when the only duty a person is supposed to have is to "feel good about himself," a lot of real guilt gets denied.

A third response is to try to find out what is making you feel guilty and stop it. By analogy, this is like feeling a sharp pain in your foot and taking your shoe off to find the source. That is the right way to deal with pain. In fact, the whole point of pain is to grab your attention. Similarly, guilt feelings are meant to make you find the source of your feelings.

As a sophomore in college I went through one of the worst depressions of my life. After a few days of real blackness, when I repeatedly cried out to God for help and seemed to get no answer, the idea occurred to me that I might be doing something wrong. Was there anything in my life that I knew quite well was sinful?

There was, as it turned out. I had been resenting a pastor of a nearby church. I had no good reason for my grudge. I just didn't like his style.

I certainly could not see any connection between that grudge and the depression I was in. But I decided that I would try to do something about it. That week I went, somewhat painfully, to a Bible study the pastor was conducting. I decided I would keep going, whether I wanted to or not, and learn to love that man. My depression vanished. As the weeks went on, I gained a great deal of insight from the Bible study. I believe that at least part of my depression was caused by guilt—the guilt of holding a grudge, of cutting myself off from another Christian.

I do not mean, by this, to start anyone on a fit of introspection. That is not healthy. We can all find plenty of sins if we are willing to look hard enough, and some of us even invent sins that aren't there at all. Don't do that. Just ask: Does God want me to do something that I have been ignoring? Is it clearly something God wants for me, something that other Christians would agree on? If so, do it. Don't pray long, weepy prayers for forgiveness. Just change your behavior.

Healing the Wounds

But you also need healing. When you have fallen down, you can make a decision not to run so carelessly any more, but you still have a scraped knee that needs healing medicine. Guilt also needs medicine: the medicine of God's forgiveness and care. Once again, 1 John helps: "If we confess our sins, he is faithful and just and will forgive us our sins and purify us from all unrighteousness" (1 John 1:9). Let us not make this a big, soul-searching issue. It is as simple as it sounds. The only requirement is that your confession be sincere: "God, I realize that I was wrong and you were right. I messed up, and I'm sorry. Will you forgive me and set me on the right track again?" That is *all* it takes, and John makes it clear that after such an action God will cleanse you from *all* your sinfulness. God doesn't clean you up 80 percent or begin a long process that may take years. There, on the spot, he cleanses you.

I find an interesting discrepancy between the way most religious people deal with guilt and the way the Bible deals with it. We are preoccupied with all the shades of guilt. Preachers sometimes urge us to search for it in our hearts. We are to find it, confess it, and then go on to find more. Some people, poor souls, are tortured with a lot of guilt; other people, lucky ones, feel very little guilt. If only the former could become more like the latter. Good news, we say. They can! If they work at it long enough they can produce a positive self-image, a deep emotional security in the fact that God loves them. Of course, they can also become better people, with less to feel guilty about!

> **"At night I wonder, 'What if I don't go to heaven with everyone else I know?' I'm a Christian, but I'm still concerned about this."**

The Bible draws a different, bigger picture. There you find no

question of adding up columns of guilt to see how much progress
you have made. It is plain: Everyone has sinned and has fallen short
of what God wants him or her to be. Then forgiveness comes with a
bang. You were 100 percent guilty, and suddenly you are 100
percent not guilty. Full and utter forgiveness is free to anyone who
wants it.

I think it is important to keep this Big Picture brilliant in our
minds. The small picture is our slow, individual advances. The Big
Picture is the explosive advance that God offers us all in his Son,
Jesus Christ. Someone like Kathy needs to be told this again and
again until it gets through.

An old story captures this message better than anything I know.
It tells about a man who has been involved in some sinful pattern for
longer than he cares to think about. How many times has he
confessed this miserable sin to God, promising that he will never do
it again? And now he comes to God again, confessing the same
thing: "Lord, I could die with shame. Again and again I have done
this thing. I confess it to you and promise that I will never, ever sin
this way again. Will you forgive me?" From heaven come the
words, "I forgive you. It is all forgotten. You are clean to start over
again."

So the man feels wonderfully free. God has forgiven him. What
more can he ask? All afternoon he revels in the belief that he will
never fall into the same sin again. And then, that very night,
temptation comes to him and he fails.

He can hardly bring himself to pray. Wasn't it just this morning
he fervently promised God he would never sin that way again? He
almost makes up his mind to ignore it, and maybe God won't notice.
But his guilty conscience gets to him, and finally he begins to talk to
God.

"God, I'm so embarrassed I can hardly talk to you. I did it
again."

"Did what?"

"That sin. The one we talked about just this morning."

"I don't remember any sin."

GAIL DENHAM

Fact #5

SOMETIMES YOU WON'T GET WHAT YOU PRAY FOR, NO MATTER HOW YOU TRY

But Often You Will, So Don't Lose Heart

by Philip Yancey

I have always been told that prayer is supposed to be a natural, spontaneous conversation between God and me. But too often in my experience it has become just one more frustration, mainly because so many of my prayers go unanswered.

I am not the only one with this problem. In fact, it is expressed beautifully in a novel that is required reading in many high school and college literature classes. *Of Human Bondage*, by Somerset Maugham, is mostly autobiographical. It includes a fictionalized incident that happened to Maugham—an incident from which his faith never recovered.

The main character, Philip, has just discovered the verse in Mark which says, "Whatever you ask in my name, believing, you will receive it." He thought immediately of his clubfoot:

He would be able to play football. His heart leaped as he saw himself running faster than any of the other boys. At the end of Easter term there were the sports, and he would be able to go in for the races; he rather fancied himself over the hurdles. It would be splendid to be like everyone else, not to be stared at curiously by new boys who did not know about his deformity, nor at the baths in summer to need incredible precautions, while he was undressing, before he could hide his foot in the water.

He prayed with all the power in his soul. No doubts assailed him. He was confident in the Word of God. And the night before he was to go back to school he went up to bed tremulous with excitement. There was snow on the ground, and Aunt Louisa had allowed herself the unaccustomed luxury of a fire in her bedroom, but in Philip's little room it was so cold that his fingers were numb, and he had great difficulty undoing his collar. His teeth chattered. The idea came to him that he must do something more unusual to attract the attention of God, and he turned back the rug which was in front of his bed so that he could kneel on the bare boards, and then it struck him that his nightshirt was a softness that might displease his Maker, so he took it off and said his prayers naked. When he got into bed he was so cold that for some time he could not sleep, but when he did, it was so soundly that Mary Ann had to shake him when she brought his hot water the next morning. She talked to him while she drew the curtains, but he did not answer; he had remembered at once that this was the morning of the miracle. His heart was filled with joy and gratitude. His first instinct was to put down his hand and feel the foot which was whole now, but to do this seemed to doubt the goodness of God. He knew that his foot was well. But at last he made up his mind, and with the toes of his right foot he just touched his left. Then he passed his toes over it.

    He limped downstairs just as Mary Ann was going into the dining room for prayers, and then he sat down to breakfast.

    "You're very quiet this morning, Philip," said Aunt Louisa presently.

Almost everyone I know has had a similar experience. Despite prayer, best friends die in car accidents; friends and bosses refuse to see your viewpoint on a certain decision; you remain badgered by a petty sin.

    The one survivor of a plane crash writes an article about how his prayers were answered, but what of all those who didn't live to write? I have read the specific promises about prayer in the Bible and tried to follow the directions. I have wanted relief from a sore throat, or I have wanted to find an important paper which got lost. But nothing happened in response to my prayers. And so I wonder, is anyone really listening? I must admit, this experience of unanswered prayer helped destroy my faith as a teenager for a while.

    The central problem with unanswered prayers is that Jesus seemed to promise there wouldn't be any. He could have said something like this: "Ladies and gentlemen, I would like to introduce to you the concept of prayer. Of course, you know that humans cannot be expected to have perfect wisdom, as God has, so there are limits to which of your prayers will be answered. Prayers will operate exactly like a suggestion box. Spell out your requests clearly to God, and I can guarantee that all requests will be carefully considered." That kind of statement about prayer I can easily live with.

    "I tell you the truth, if you have faith and do not doubt . . . you can say to this mountain, 'Go, throw yourself into the sea,' and it will be done. If you believe,

you will receive whatever you ask for in prayer" (Matthew 21:21, 22).

*"Again, I tell you that if two of you on earth agree
about anything you ask for, it will be done for you by my
Father in heaven"* (Matthew 18:19).

*"You may ask me for anything in my name, and I
will do it"* (John 14:14).

Those are just a few of the strong statements in the New
Testament. Others abound, such as John 16:23–27 and Mark 11:24.
If you are interested, look them up. They prove to me that I can't
squirm out of this sticky problem by saying, "Jesus didn't really
promise prayer would be answered." All those claims are lavishly
made. The Bible is not fuzzy on this issue.

A CLOSER LOOK

So what is the solution to this problem of unanswered prayer?
By studying each of the major sections of the Bible which contain
the promises, I have learned some facts which help me understand
the matter. The whole subject is still mysterious and slightly
muddled, but my bitterness over unanswered prayer has faded as I
have grown to understand the role of prayer in the Christian life.
Here are three of the key factors:

1. *Jesus' statements, taken at face value, are impossible, so we have
to search for a deeper meaning behind them.* Why are they impossible?
Because people pray for contradictory requests, and God cannot
answer both requests. In the Civil War godly men like Abraham
Lincoln, Stonewall Jackson, and Robert E. Lee all prayed for
victory earnestly and frequently. But the North and South couldn't
both win!

If Oral Roberts University plays Wheaton College in basketball,
both teams might pray for victory. But I can guarantee that one
team will not get the answer it prefers!

There is an even stronger illustration: Jesus did not get what he prayed for in Gethsemane. He asked God to please find some other way, to spare him the pain, if it was his will (Mark 14:32–42). Often this basic fact is left out of Christian teaching on prayer. Our model for all of life, the perfect Man with perfect faith who taught us how to pray, was killed even though he asked God his Father to spare him! Obviously, some prayers get turned down no matter how faith-filled we are.

Paul had a similar problem, stemming from a physical ailment he called his "thorn in the flesh" (see 2 Corinthians 12:7–9). Despite three pleas to God to take the pain away, Paul's request was denied. Therefore, I conclude that what Jesus said cannot be applied to all prayers at all times.

"I've prayed and asked God to help or heal people, but they just continue to be sick. I feel like I'm praying to the air."

2. *Jesus directed each of his strong statements about prayer to a specific group of people: the disciples.* During his time on earth Jesus selected twelve men to carry on his ministry after his death. These were special people, given special tasks by God. (They were so select that when the church decided which writings should be included in the New Testament, they included those written by the disciples almost automatically.)

Could it be that Jesus gave his disciples certain rights and privileges in prayer that don't apply to all Christians in the same degree? After all, who of us can duplicate Peter's miracles or John's inspired writings?

The Gospel writers do not explicitly say, "These commands apply to the disciples only," but they do tell us, in each case, that Jesus was talking to his twelve disciples, not a large crowd.

Frankly, I don't know how far to carry this point. But perhaps it could help explain the sweeping nature of Jesus' promises.

Perhaps he was investing in the disciples a specific gift of boldness and insight into God's will. They were mature men who had spent three years learning directly from Jesus; chances are they would have a good idea of which prayers would further God's purpose on earth and which would be capricious (of a "help our team win" category).

Interestingly, in such passages as 1 John 5:14–15, John, writing to a large group, carefully says that "if we ask anything according to his will, he hears us." That phrase "according to his will" is a key qualification, I believe.

Jesus Focused on the Father

3. *Since it was Jesus who made the sweeping claims about prayer, I looked carefully at the kind of prayers he prayed.* One trend surprised me. I had always viewed prayers as focused on and determined by me, the person praying. But Jesus' prayers showed that the focus ought to be on the Father, the one prayed to. Jesus used prayer as a time to commune with the Father, to refresh himself in God's will, to ask for strength. He also used it to thank God for the world and to mention his friends who had needs. It was a conversation, not a shopping list.

Charlie Shedd calls prayer "an inner dialogue with your best friend." I had instead viewed it as a magic wand I could wave to make God do what I wanted. I am not the one in charge of prayer, however; God is.

Many people share the misconception I once had. For example, Mark Twain, who was bothered by unanswered prayer, expressed the dilemma in *Huckleberry Finn.* Huck got a lesson from Miss Watson in prayer.

> *She told me to pray every day, and whatever I asked for I would get it. But it warn't so. I tried it. Once I got a fishline but no hooks. It warn't any good to me without hooks. I tried for the hooks three or four times,*

but somehow I couldn't make it work. By and by one day I asked Miss Watson to try for me, but she said I was a fool. She never told me why. I couldn't make it out no way.

I set down one time back in the woods and had a long think about it. I says to myself, "If a body can get anything they pray for, why don't Deacon Winn get back the money he lost on pork? Why don't the widow get back her silver snuffbox that was stolen? Why can't Miss Watson fat up? No! says I to myself, there ain't nothing in it."

Obviously, Huck wanted a genie in a bottle who would perform his wishes on command, not a God who would be Lord of his life. Faith, to him, was a mental flex to get what he wanted. But faith should be in God, trusting his love and willingness to respond wisely.

DIFFERENT TYPES OF REQUESTS

As I went through the Bible examining prayers, I couldn't help notice that requests are a small part of prayer. Some prayer is worship, some repentance, some praise. The Psalms, for example, are a series of prayers set to poetry. Read through them and notice how few of them are essentially request prayers. Prayer is not a vending machine that spits out the appropriate reward. It is a call to a loving Father to help us.

The motive of prayer cannot be "What can I get?" That's magic. It has to be, "God, I believe this is your will, but it's beyond my power. Can you help me?" In the Lord's Prayer, Jesus expressed it this way, "Thy kingdom come, thy will be done."

The Bible is clear that God hears our prayers, even the ones that don't get answered as we would like. He carefully considers the most absurd and selfish requests. When children ask foolish things of wise parents—such as, "May I stay up to watch the late, late show?" or "Will you let me drive even though I'm only twelve?"—they don't always get their way. Usually the parents know better what is good for the child.

While studying the request prayers which are illustrated in the Bible, I noticed that even their styles differ greatly. I observed at least three kinds:

1. *The humble, submissive-to-the-will-of-God request like Jesus prayed in Gethsemane before he was crucified.* That prayer takes deep trust in God, because we are actually saying, "I honestly want to do what you want me to do." In Jesus' case, that meant submitting to death. These prayers usually have the tag, "If it be your will," and in fact some Christians believe it is proper to pray all prayers with that attitude.

2. *The unusual prayers made by people with simple faith who really believe God will honor them.* Often young Christians make requests for miraculous healing, huge amounts of money, supernatural guidance. And the older Christians have a point: taken to its extreme, this type of faith can result in tragedy. Every so often newspapers carry stories of religious parents whose children die after they refuse to let them be treated for leukemia or some other serious illness. (Remember Somerset Maugham, who lost his faith when he gambled on a miracle.) Yet if you study the Bible, you find a place for bold, childlike faith. Jesus praised such faith when he saw it in the centurion (Luke 7). Many of his parables about prayer encouraged audacious requests.

These bold prayers puzzle me. Why do some people's prayers get answered with regularity, while mine sputter along? At various times in my Christian life I have thought of prayer as a spiritual muscle. I saw faith as similar to doing push-ups: if you work hard every day, soon you will get the reward of bulging arm muscles and have more strength to do what you want.

But prayer apparently doesn't work quite that way. Faith is not something I can muster up by concentrating hard, like a yoga meditation. I know that because some of the most spectacular answers to prayer I have seen occur to brand-new Christians who are "just ignorant and naive enough" to believe that God really will perform a miracle for them. God seems to honor that enthusiastic young faith.

3. *The large requests made when people are praying for something they are almost sure is the will of God.* Thus Jesus and his followers could pray with complete confidence for physical healing because they were so in touch with God they knew it to be his will. For us to pray with such confidence we should, like them, have good reasons to believe the answer we want is closely aligned with God's will. This last category seems to me to be the goal for mature Christians, though I find most of my request prayers fall into the first category.

Perhaps that is because God's will is complex and hard to grasp. He is concerned not only for us personally, but for the whole universe. Regardless of how we categorize our prayers, we cannot take Scripture verses and try to read them as a money-back guarantee that God will answer any prayer. Charlie Shedd expresses it this way: "Our great, wonderful, loving God has answers we don't know anything about. This is where faith comes in. We have to believe that he means it when he says, 'Our lives are eternal. What you see happening here is just the backside of the rug. It isn't so beautiful on this side as it is on the finished side. You have to believe me that under all the circumstances, I know what's best.' About a thousand years from now you will probably say, 'Hey, I see!'"

Paul said, "And we know that in all things God works for the good of those who love him, who have been called according to his purpose" (Romans 8:28). Joni Eareckson experienced this goodness after a diving accident left her paralyzed. Her prayers for healing were not answered, but God is now using her life story in books and a movie to encourage the faith of millions. Her pain did work out for the cause of good.

An enormous warfare between good and evil is raging around us and in us. Prayer offers a few minutes for us to loudly show we are on the side of good. We are linked up with God's concerns and God's will. We make contact with our King.

PRAYER AND FAITH

Faith is not a formula to unlock God's well-kept secret. It is a trust in God, whether he does things I want or lets me endure hard times. In Hebrews 11, sometimes called the "Faith Hall of Fame," some of the giants of the faith hardly got the results they wanted. Some were rescued from floods and pharaohs and lions. But right along with them were others who were beaten to death, lashed with whips, or sawed in two.

Both groups had powerful faith, which is hailed as a model for us. Faith didn't necessarily remove their problems, but it won God's praise and reward. Faith is not an inflatable quantity you can pump up to get God's attention. It is a quality of trust that takes us outside ourselves into God's desires on earth.

Often, when it looks as if one of my requests has been turned down, God answers it indirectly. The mother of a great Christian leader, Augustine, experienced this. Monica prayed all night that God would stop her son from going to Italy because she wanted him to become a Christian. He tricked her and sailed away. It seemed her prayers had gone unheard. But in Italy Augustine was converted. God is loving and wise, and he can deny our prayers in order to bring even greater blessing to us.

Discussions on prayer tend to get complex and confusing. Perhaps that is why the Bible doesn't outline the process in detail, showing us all the fine points and mysteries of prayer. Rather, we are beckoned to come to God in prayer as a child, setting aside our doubts. Why did Jesus use such extravagant promises? I don't fully know. Maybe it was to push us toward extravagant faith.

Jesus said, "Which of you fathers, if your son asks for a fish, will give him a snake instead? Or if he asks for an egg, will give him a scorpion? If you then, though you are evil, know how to give good gifts to your children, how much more will your Father in heaven give the Holy Spirit to those who ask him!" (Luke 11:11–13).

In the final analysis it is not so amazing that God denies some of my requests. What is amazing is that he listens to me at all! Every prayer ends up in God's active file. My role is to flood him with requests and then commit to him the trust that accepts his answers.

GAIL DENHAM

Fact #6

AT TIMES THE BIBLE WILL SEEM DRY AS DUST

*But Go to Work,
and the Dust Can
Spring Forth Life*

by Tim Stafford

Christians believe that the Bible is the best book ever written—a gift to us from God himself. The Bible doesn't merely tell us *about* God, it is a channel for him to come directly to us. Through the Bible we can meet God and hear his voice speaking to us.

This belief, while well-founded, sets people up for some unsettling surprises. A Gallup Poll revealed that the majority of Americans believe the Bible to be divinely inspired. Yet only a small percentage of those same Americans could name four of the Ten Commandments or other equally basic Bible facts. For the majority, the Bible sits somewhere on a shelf, impressive to look at, but unread.

Even committed Christians fail. In a survey initiated by *Campus Life* magazine, young Christians repeatedly mentioned their guilt for not reading the Bible consistently. They believed in the Bible. They expected to find help there. They saw it as a holy book. But they did not read the Bible nearly so often as they thought they should, and this frustrating paradox was a major reason for them to doubt their faith.

After all, if God really wants to speak to you, and makes himself available to you every day, and yet you never "find time" to listen to his voice—what kind of Christian are you?

SECRETS ABOUT THE BIBLE

Should this paradox cause people to doubt their faith? I don't think so. The paradox doesn't usually come from a lack of real belief. It comes, I think, from some unrealistic expectations about the Bible.

In most churches, people talk about the great benefits of reading the Bible. They don't say much about how hard that reading can be. People openly tell about the times when the Bible encouraged, corrected, or inspired them. They keep secret the times when the Bible seemed as appetizing as yesterday's coffee.

I'm quite sure that most Christians struggle all through their lives to read and understand the Bible. Few if any find it enjoyable all the time. They rarely mention this, especially to younger Christians, for fear it would discourage them. Actually, by keeping the difficulty of the Bible a secret they increase others' guilty frustration. Young Christians especially think there must be something wrong with them if they don't find the Bible a consistent inspiration.

For several years I have been involved with a project meant to overcome barriers to Bible reading. (The result of our work: *The NIV Student Bible*.) We used modern research techniques to try to find an answer to the question, "What keeps you from reading the Bible?" The encouraging news was that the vast majority of young Christians had a very high view of the Scripture. They expected good things from the Bible. The discouraging news was that very few of them found those good things on a consistent basis. Only a small percentage of them could claim they read the Bible on anything close to a regular basis. When asked why, they gave answers that fell into three categories: "I get discouraged," "I can't understand it," "I can't find anything."

"I Get Discouraged"

Simple discouragement is by far the most common reason for not reading the Bible. Most of the people in our research felt guilty:

Every experiment they had tried in Bible reading had ended in failure.

The Bible is a big book, over one thousand pages long. How many people have read any other one thousand-page book? People who start with Genesis, planning to read through the whole Bible, very often get bogged down somewhere around Numbers or Deuteronomy. Fatigue sets in. I would guess that about the same number who complete *War and Peace* also finish the Bible.

A great many more people never even start. Their busy schedules and their limited confidence keep them from starting a project they feel sure they'll fail to complete. Instead, they read occasionally from familiar passages like Philippians or the Psalms. But to venture out into unfamiliar books—they wouldn't know where to begin.

"I Can't Understand It"

Lack of basic understanding creates a second major barrier to Bible reading. Today many readers have grown up with very little exposure to the Bible. They may never have heard of Goliath or Abraham. Often they ask, "What is the point of reading about spears and chariots and village wells and leprosy?"

Because it was written several thousand years ago, the Bible presents a culture gap: it uses hard-to-pronounce names and refers to many outdated customs. For most readers, the Bible is the most ancient book in their library. They find it hard and confusing to read Shakespeare—and Shakespeare is only a fraction as old as the Bible.

"I Can't Find Anything"

"I spend so much time just flipping through the Bible looking for something," many people say. Bible readers are often looking for help on specific issues—but they don't know where to find it. Everybody has heard of something from the Bible: The Ten

Commandments, the Golden Rule, the story of Daniel in the lions' den. But how do you know where to look for them? The Bible is too large just to flip through on a random search.

Until you have run into these three problems, you really don't know much about the Bible. The Bible is not an easy read. But who said it should be?

Because the Bible is a holy book, a gift from God, we sometimes act as though it is not a book at all. It becomes a magical symbol: a black cover or gilt edges set it apart. In reality, the Bible's holiness doesn't come from its appearance. It comes from its ability to communicate the Word of God to us. It does this in much the same way that other books do: we have to read and understand. Our misconceptions and mistaken expectations often just get in the way. I don't have anything against black covers or gilt edges. But I do object to the misconceptions that damage Christians' ability to read and understand.

> **"I try reading the Bible, but usually I just end up more confused than when I started. Why does it have to be so hard to understand?"**

Misconception #1: The Bible is an inspirational book. The Bible is inspiring, of course. "Inspire" comes from a Latin word meaning "breathe." The Bible inspires by breathing new life into us, the life of the Holy Spirit of God. But how does the Bible do it? Not in the way that "inspirational" books do.

"Inspirational" books are usually full of poetic encouragement. They make you feel great. They bring a catch to your throat and tears to your eyes. Usually you can pick up an inspirational book at any point, read a page or two, and find yourself emotionally moved. The Bible is not inspirational in this sense. Oh, it is in places. But a great deal of it isn't. Most of it isn't pitched at your emotions at all, but at your mind. The Bible "inspires" primarily by reforming and teaching. Some of that is downright unpleasant, especially where it tells you what you are doing wrong and warns you of the consequences.

If you do go to the Bible thinking it is "inspirational reading," you will often be disappointed, and you will eventually restrict your reading to just a few small parts of the Bible, such as the Psalms (though not all the Psalms, either—some are far from "inspirational"). On the other hand, if you go to the Bible expecting to learn what God is doing in the world and what he expects of you, you will be inspired. You will learn what God is all about, and that will breathe "new life" into you.

Misconception #2: The Bible is a collection of wonderful verses. I think this misconception comes partly from the way the Bible is used in sermons. Many pastors, knowing the Bible well, quote from a variety of verses scattered through the Bible. Each one of these is a gem. Some Bibles also list verses you can look at for help in times of trouble, discouragement, temptation, and other trials.

Unfortunately, some people get the idea that the Bible is a treasury of great and inspiring fragments. Unfortunately, though they hunt for them, they rarely find them. The Bible is not a religious version of *Bartlett's Quotations*, providing raw material for greeting cards and bumper stickers. It happens to have some great quotes in it, but if you read the book just to find the great quotes, you will miss the author's point.

To understand God's Word, you need to read it paragraph by paragraph, chapter by chapter, book by book. You need to get a sense of the whole story. This means that you have to read long passages. You can't just look for a Thought for the Day. But why should we expect any different? Our God is a big God. He has a big story to tell. You can't fit him on a bumper sticker.

Misconception #3: You don't need any help to understand the Bible. This idea probably developed out of the Reformation, which rebelled—rightly, I think—against church leaders suggesting that ordinary people couldn't read the Bible and understand God's message for themselves. God's Word speaks to people at many levels of sophistication, and often a very uneducated person can teach someone with a Ph.D. Listening to God's voice doesn't require a graduate degree.

But this fact seems to encourage some people to think that ideally you should take the Bible into the privacy of your room, open it up, and let God speak to you in a way that he speaks to no one else. In a mysterious way, you will be given unexplainable secrets of understanding.

God's Spirit does have some personal messages for you. But the more clearly you understand the Bible, the more clearly the Spirit can speak through it. You understand the Bible just as you understand most books—first by reading it, then by discussing it with others, and finally by being taught about it by people who have studied the book much longer than you have. This is particularly true of an ancient book dealing with unfamiliar customs and geography.

Most people who successfully read the Bible get help. A lot of them are in a Bible study group. Many use Bible study guides, commentaries, Bible dictionaries, or have Bibles with explanatory notes. These aids do not interfere with the process by which God's Spirit speaks to us. They assist.

PRACTICAL SOLUTIONS

The Bible is a book to be mastered; it requires the full commitment of your whole self: body, mind, and spirit. Your body comes into it as you discipline yourself to sit still and read, just as you discipline yourself to do your homework. Your mind comes into it as you grapple to understand, just as you grapple with mathematics or any other difficult subject. Your spirit comes into it as you submit to the truth as God gives it. God calls all of you, and responding to his call is a lifelong challenge.

Yet it is utterly unlike mathematics homework. Does reading the Bible sound grim? It isn't. As you respond to God, he breathes new life into you. Increasingly, you want to do what he says. Increasingly, you love his Word—the actual words in the Bible, as well as the way God uses them in your life. Talk to someone who's run a marathon or climbed a mountain and you'll get the idea. They may say it was the hardest thing they ever did. But the pride in achievement and the sense of being changed forever by the experience override the difficulty.

Practically speaking, you need help if you are to succeed at reading the Bible. It's like training for a marathon: Only you can do it, but some ways are easier than others.

First, you need a Bible in a modern translation. Lots of people have the idea that the Bible sounds "more like the Bible" in the King James Version. The King James is a great translation, but it is as ancient as Shakespeare. Most people can't understand it easily. The Bible really sounds "more like the Bible" when you read and understand it—not when you like the way the words vibrate against your eardrums. Many newer translations are at least as accurate as the King James, and they are far easier to understand.

Second, you need a realistic system for reading the Bible. Don't start at Genesis and try to work your way through. Don't aimlessly flip through the Bible looking for "good stuff." Start with two or three of the basic books in the New Testament, such as Luke (an account of Jesus' life) and Ephesians. When you've read and understood them pretty well, ask a pastor or someone you trust for recommendations of what to read next.

A number of excellent systems for reading the whole Bible exist. Unfortunately, most of them ask you to read several chapters a day, and they concentrate on getting through the whole Bible. A beginning Bible reader should probably not try to read much more than one chapter a day, and he or she should concentrate on some of the books in the Bible that are easiest to understand. Later on, you can go on to do more.

Third, you need to develop a consistent time when you read the Bible each day. This isn't a moral issue—God doesn't command you to have a "quiet time." It's a practical issue. The Bible is such a long book that only regular reading, year after year, will enable you to know it well. Daily reading helps you take its wisdom into daily life. Bit by bit, God's Word becomes part of your thinking. Very few people spontaneously read the Bible every day. Most people must make it a habit at a particular time, day in, day out.

Fourth, you should seek out other Christians who can help you understand the Bible. Many churches and Christian organizations have Bible study programs where small groups of people study the Bible together. These can help tremendously, especially where a well-trained leader leads the group.

Fifth, it is a good idea to spend some money for materials to help you understand the Bible. A Christian bookstore can provide you with many options:

> *Bible Study Guides* take you through certain books of the Bible, or through certain themes. You can hardly work your way through one of these fill-in-the-blank booklets without learning something.
>
> *Study Bibles* contain footnotes and other explanatory helps. When you buy a study Bible, don't be impressed by the sheer volume and complexity of the helps. Read some of the explanations and make sure that you will really understand them. It's better to buy a simple one you will really use than an impressive one that confuses you.
>
> *A Bible Dictionary* is really more of an encyclopedia (in one volume) than a dictionary. Any subject you are interested in—"David," "faith," "prophecy"—will get a brief but thorough explanation. All the places, people, and books of the Bible get covered.
>
> *A Concordance* tells you where to find all the verses that use a particular word. If you're interested in "faith," all the times the Bible uses that word will be listed. A concordance is particularly useful if you want to study a subject in depth.

You don't need all of these helps. You don't necessarily need any of them. But they can help in a difficult task.

The Disturbing Word Difficult

Difficult? Lots of people feel disturbed by that word *difficult*. It makes reading the Bible sound as attractive as writing a term paper. Many people want reading the Bible to be as relaxing as a warm bath. It isn't. Parts of it are. Overall, it's more like training for sports. It feels great when you do it. But it is hard work.

Consider the alternatives. You can hold on to your misconceptions about what the Bible should be like—and you can keep right on feeling guilty, and short of the breath of God.

Or you can accept the Bible for what it is—a long, challenging book that requires all you have, during all your life. If you accept this challenge, you can approach it intelligently, with commitment, and succeed. God will speak to you through his Word, and the speech will grow clearer and clearer.

CLEO FREELANCE PHOTO

Fact #7

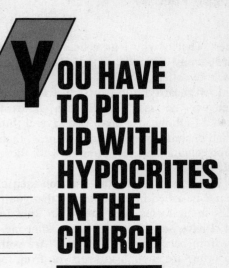

YOU HAVE TO PUT UP WITH HYPOCRITES IN THE CHURCH

But You Begin to Understand How Gracious God Is

by Tim Stafford

I shall call him Mr. Thomas. He seldom missed church. He always prayed longer than anyone else and was most concerned about the "spiritual" dimensions of any problem. Yet he had cheated his relatives out of the family business, was a snoop, a liar, and, to top it all off, overweight. Though I haven't seen him in years, I would still find it hard to enjoy shaking hands with him. He exuded slime. When I hear the word *hypocrite* I think of him.

Hypocrites are an easy excuse. Ask someone why he doesn't go to church, for instance, and you are likely to hear, "Because the church is full of hypocrites."

That answer helps him avoid saying, "Because I don't want to get up Sunday mornings" or "Because I don't believe in God the way Christians do" or "Because I like my life the way it is and don't want to get close to something that might make me change." Any of these three, and plenty of others, would be honest reasons.

But someone who says the church is full of hypocrites puts his questioner on the defensive and doesn't have to deal with the real issues. That is why I have heard this excuse so often. I have also heard many Christians stumble and hedge defensively when somebody offers it.

I overheard a non-Christian friend try a variation of it. When asked why he wasn't a Christian, he explained that he had been raised a Catholic. He described several things wrong with the nuns he had encountered: their uptightness, their severity, their mumbo-jumbo religion. He was hung up with those nuns; that was why, he said, he wasn't a Christian.

The person asking the question then broke into a laugh. "You mean," he asked incredulously, "that you're going to let a few little ladies in uniforms keep you from knowing God?" Since I heard that, I have had an answer when someone tells me hypocrites keep him from becoming a Christian. "Are you trying to say that a few hypocrites are enough to keep you from meeting God personally?"

That helps deal with the excuse, leaving you free to talk about genuine issues. But aren't there times when hypocrites are a genuine issue? For most people they are just an excuse, but are they always? Even as a Christian I am bothered by the existence of hypocrites— people like Mr. Thomas. They raise troublesome questions. If Christianity is so wonderful, why aren't Christians more wonderful people?

Why is it you find liars in the same building where truth is exalted week after week? Why does the religion that changes lives have phonies everywhere? It's as shocking as going into a presidential candidate's headquarters and finding that his workers plan to vote against him. The insincerity surrounding the candidate makes you doubt the candidate himself.

It is the real question, not the excuse, that I want to deal with here. Why are there hypocritical Christians, and what are we supposed to do with them?

Behind the Counterfeit

A hypocrite might be called a counterfeit Christian, and that term sheds light. Why do people counterfeit something? Only because that something is valuable. No one counterfeits a traffic ticket. No one fakes a bad report card. Only more valuable objects are counterfeited: things like twenty-dollar bills.

People will pretend to be rich. They will fake being university professors or football players. They will not usually pretend to be child beaters.

People often pretend to know God intimately. Why? Because knowing God is such a valuable thing they want people to think they do. In a way, the presence of hypocrites demonstrates how desirable real Christianity is.

A generation or two ago, people would join the church because that was what all decent people did. Today, you don't lose respect if you don't go to church or claim to be a Christian. The only reason to be a hypocritical Christian is that you think knowing God is valuable. I do not mean that hypocrites consciously calculate how to "counterfeit" Christianity. What is a hypocrite? Hypocrites are those trying to gain respect from every group they're in. Around Christians they act spiritual, because that is what they think will make them admired. Around other circles they act unspiritual, because that

"A lot of the Christian kids here at school talk real holy and piously and say all the right words, but then they gossip about someone or act like hot shots. The thing that gets me is that I do it too."

will win them another kind of admiration or power. They are chameleons, colored by their environment. Not having enough character to be themselves, they are forced to try to live up to a set of contradictory standards.

Of course, they gain only misery. They don't fool many people for long. Christians are not the only ones disgusted by a hypocrite;

even those who live unspiritually all the time look down on someone who tries to have it both ways.

So when I recognize a hypocrite, I have learned that the proper attitude is sadness. I am seeing a person who doesn't know who he really is. He is too weak to be consistent, and he is probably miserable.

Yet it is one thing to know sadness is the proper attitude, and another to use it with love. I think of Mr. Thomas again. I have a hard enough time loving family and friends. How am I to love this man who is so repulsively false?

The only way is to see deeper into him: to see the misery in his soul, and also to see somehow the real person buried under piles of lies and fears. Somewhere inside must be the person God made.

But how can I ignore all the obvious faults in a Mr. Thomas? How can I discover the person God meant him to be if he can't discover it himself? I find that I understand someone like him only when I examine my own life carefully. When I look deeply into my own soul I discover that I am not much better than Mr. Thomas.

It's All in the Attitude

Hypocrites say they believe one thing but live another. By that standard I am a hypocrite, and so are you. In fact, everyone who claims to a Christian is in one sense a hypocrite. Did not Jesus tell us, "You shall love the Lord your God with all your mind, soul and strength, and your neighbor as yourself"? And don't we agree that those words are the standard for life? But none of us lives up to those words. The greatest difference between me and Mr. Thomas is not whether I live up to my beliefs; on that score I am a failure too. The difference is in our attitude toward the failure.

Jesus once told a story about two men who prayed. The first man, a hypocritical religious leader, thanked God for the moral character he lived, which was considerably above the norm. The other man, a notorious crook, was so ashamed of himself he could barely speak to God. He did not thank God for anything. All he asked for was mercy. Jesus commented that the second man, not the first, was pleasing to God.

The man was pleasing not because he had sinned less, but because of his humble attitude. He knew his faults, and he didn't try to hide them.

Now, which of those two men do you think might have been cynical about a church where he could find hypocrites? The first man, obviously. He would not think of himself as a hypocrite—he lived a good life and was proud of it. He looked down on those who abused the Ten Commandments. He would consider himself too good to attend a church of hypocrites.

You can't imagine that attitude in the second man. He was so aware of his own faults that it never occurred to him to be offended by other people's. It is this attitude that pleases God, Jesus says.

When I hear the story, I try to place myself in it. When I am upset about hypocrites, am I not like the first man? But when I look deep into myself and see how far my own hypocrisy goes, I become more like the second man. Then, I don't have the courage (or the desire) to sneer at others—even at Mr. Thomas.

Each of us comes to Jesus as a starving man after bread. What does it say about me if I turn around to sneer at other starving men who don't yet know where the bread is?

But . . . in Church?

Of course, one big obstacle to accepting hypocrites is that we find them in church. If I meet someone who is dishonest and mean in the grocery store I am not going to spit on him. But aren't Christians supposed to be different? Doesn't the Bible call Christians holy people? If so, why do churches tolerate hypocrites?

The answer is that most churches try not to. That is, they say loud and clear, almost every week, that dishonesty and selfishness keep us from really living. They encourage people to confront what is wrong with their lives. Some churches will take the extreme measure of expelling someone who consistently, outwardly sins and won't admit it and change.

It is difficult to see what more a church could do. Is there a hypocrisy test we could give everyone? That begins to sound like the Inquisition. Frankly, I wouldn't want anybody else testing *my* hypocrisy. And I don't feel competent to judge anyone else's. Who really knows another person's heart? How can we tell what a person thinks when he's alone? We can evaluate what someone does, but how can we evaluate his sincerity? I would much rather leave that sort of judging to God. If I understand the Bible correctly, some of his judgments will turn out to be surprising to us.

Beyond that, I have to ask what a church is supposed to be. Are we to separate out the pure people and pack them into a building once a week? Or are we to have open doors to those whose lives are inconsistent and troubled?

The Bible calls Christians holy, but is that because they have resolved all hypocrisy and inconsistency in their lives? Not in my case. My only claim to "holiness" is that, time and time again, I bring my hypocrisies and inconsistencies to Jesus and allow him to forgive and renew me. That, I think is all the holiness any of us will reach on earth.

I am thinking of Mr. Thomas again. He is a slimy character, but

"Sometimes I feel like Christianity is all a big joke because of the way my parents act. I get yelled at every Sunday on the way to church and I get all upset. Then my dad walks into church with a big smile, while I go to Sunday school hating him and everything about the church."

perhaps God has been working to change him. I don't know what he was like twenty years ago; it may be he had a long way to come. I can't compare his morality with someone else's. I can only hope that he is better than he would be without God at all.

Nor do I know what Mr. Thomas is thinking inside. Maybe a sense of crisis is right now bringing him to the brink of change. I would not want to be the one who stepped in and condemned him the day before he gave in to God's urging.

But even if he never changes, what will that prove except that God wants us to be free? He wants an army of volunteers, not draftees. He will allow Mr. Thomas—or me—to go on in hypocrisy. He allows each of us the dignity to make up his or her own mind. God's only force is the subtle, steady pressure of his Spirit on our minds.

God could force each of us today to come to terms with everything contradictory inside. If he did, I doubt many of us would have the strength to go on calling ourselves Christians. Instead, he brings our faults to us one at a time, and if we want to ignore them, we can. Since God allows freedom, there will always be hypocrites.

But when we do change our minds and let God's rule operate in our lives, he makes us free. We are free, most of all, to stop pretending that we have no problems. A hypocrite is someone hiding his problems inside, pretending they don't exist. A Christian is someone free enough to let his problems out and to give them each day to God.

MICHAEL SILUK

Fact #8

SOMETIMES THE BIGGEST CHRISTIANS MAKE YOU FEEL FARTHEST FROM GOD

But Grace Is Jesus' Antidote

by Philip Yancey

We've talked about hypocrites—people who act very religious but live in a way that contradicts the faith they claim. They make an obvious stumbling block for many young Christians.

Another kind of people, the legalists, may make just the opposite impression on you. You are likely to be terrifically impressed by their rigorous faith. These super-dedicated Christians seem to know all the answers. And they make no compromises. They live strictly and pour their lives into Christian concerns. They can inspire you.

Yet you may grow convinced, eventually, that they drive you away from God. Perhaps you will find that you simply can't live up to the rules that they insist on. Or perhaps you will simply sense harshness underneath their religiosity. You may feel in their attitudes more than in their words that they have grown proud, losing a sense of their dependence on Christ and his grace. Yet, if you are typical, you will find it hard to put your finger on what is wrong. They seem so holy! So sincere! So dedicated! I, too, struggled for years to understand whether there was something wrong with these people's faith in God—or whether the problem lay with me. One strange character named Josh helped me put it into perspective.

At a small group meeting in church I met him: a strange, lonely guy. Josh would seldom look you straight in the face; he stared down, or sometimes over your shoulder into the distance. He always looked nervous, as if he were about to clear his throat. Josh said little, and I had tried to loosen him up by inviting him to the group.

The discussion that night was on what makes a Christian unique. One man mentioned how Christians are the only ones who have a reason for hope. The rest of the world, he said, has to spend life depressed since they can't be sure of an afterlife.

A woman talked about how Christians have so much happiness and peace. Another, a young girl, mentioned that Christians have higher standards than other people.

Josh sat silently through the discussion, occasionally scraping his feet in imaginary shapes on the floor. Later, when I asked him about the evening, he didn't look up. He said, "Well, I always thought Christians were people who admitted they were sinners. The rest of us weren't supposed to have discovered that yet. But tonight it seemed to me these folks were proud of their religion. It's like they think they're superior to me or something."

Josh's words cut deeply. I had sat smugly through the meeting, proud of my articulate friends with all the answers. But Josh helped me begin to see that I had forgotten about the word *grace*.

PEOPLE WHO MADE JESUS ANGRY

Jesus Christ knew various crooked people when he was on earth: sneaky tax collectors, streetwalkers, thieves, ruthless soldiers. But as he traveled the streets of Jerusalem and other Jewish towns, one group particularly seemed to get under his skin. He singled them out for his strongest attacks. "Snakes!" he called them. "Tangle of vipers! Fools! Hypocrites! Blind guides! Whitewashed tombs!"

Strangely, the people who made Jesus livid with anger were the ones the press might call Bible-Belt fundamentalists today. This group, the Pharisees, devoted their lives to following God. They gave away an exact tithe, obeyed every minute law in the Old Testament, and sent out missionaries to gain new converts. There was almost no sexual sin or violent crime among the Pharisees. Weren't the Pharisees the type Jesus should have felt most comfortable with?

His reaction shows how seriously he viewed legalism. The Pharisees had the idea that we earn God's acceptance by following a list of definable, external rules. Legalism is especially dangerous because on the outside it looks so respectable. It creates clean-cut, pure, pious followers of God.

> **"When you become a Christian, it's as if you sign a contract, and you're supposed to know all the fine print. If you don't, you'd better learn it fast."**

I first ran into legalism in an extremely conservative church when growing up in Atlanta, Georgia. It took only one month of attendance to figure out what the list of "don'ts" were in that church. The list included dancing, cardplaying, smoking, drinking, civil rights, movies, rock music, long hair, games on Sunday, dice games, mini-skirts, swimming with the other sex, and dating blacks or Hispanics. If you stayed away from all those evils and carried a Bible you were automatically accepted into the group.

Later in a Bible college in the South, I ran into a new list of rules. There, integration was supported (but still no interracial dating, and to stay on the safe side, the one resident black student roomed with the one resident Puerto Rican). Bowling, one of the Atlanta church youth group's favorite activities, was frowned on because some bowling alleys served liquor. Who would know whether you went there to bowl or to drink? Roller skating was forbidden, because skaters had the pernicious habit of holding hands while they skated, and besides, skating looked suspiciously like dancing.

The real hang-up at the Bible college seemed to be with sex. So innocent an act as a guy holding hands with a girl was banned. Handholders or especially kissers who were caught by a dean were quickly up on restriction or dismissed from school. One teacher went so far as to rail in class against lipstick, which to him was a sign of harlotry.

Looking back, the Bible college rules seem sort of humorous. (They were enforced with an iron fist and rarely seemed humorous at the time.) The rules may have been excessive, but were they actually harmful? They all sound pretty innocent, hardly deserving of strong words like those Jesus leveled at the Pharisees. I would probably merely view them as a sort of joke, if it were not for the concern Jesus obviously had. What made him speak so strongly?

The Pharisees were dangerous, I believe, because they were so close to the truth. They believed in holiness, as God does, but they wanted the privilege of defining it. They snobbishly rejected any believers who did not follow their strict rules. They were so close to the truth that they could easily lead others astray—to confuse the truth with a close substitute. The Pharisees had a list of rules that you could follow to gain God's acceptance; God never had to give you a thing except his seal of approval. Jesus wanted people to find holiness as a gift from God.

In some ways the legalists I met in Atlanta and Bible college were unlike the Pharisees. Few of them would have said that following their rules would earn God's acceptance. Yet they *acted* as if the rules were so important that God himself stood behind them. And they, too, tended to rate how "spiritual" people were according to their rules.

Four Subtle Dangers

Almost every Christian group has its own form of legalism. The dangers are so subtle that Jesus focused on them, spelling out the problems with legalism in Luke 11 and Matthew 23. They can be summarized this way:

1. *Legalism can be practiced for show.* When Pharisees prayed long hours, they made sure they were out on a street corner to be noticed. They wore unusual clothing to call attention to how religious they were. The groups I was in never went so far as to require a specific uniform, as the Pharisees did, but I must admit the lipstickless, jewelryless, skirt-dragging Bible college girls were easy to spot. The danger here, Jesus warned, is that most outer looks could cover up a lot of hidden problems that need dealing with. In my hall at Bible college there were guys who had severe problems with guilt over masturbation, anger with parents and authorities, racial discrimination, hatred of some political groups. Somehow those things stayed undercover most of the time. We paid more attention to the visible things; we had no choice—a slip-up could get us expelled.

Jesus' first warning was against the pride that legalism frequently produces. By obeying all the rules, the Pharisees began believing they really were morally superior to other people. At Bible college I noticed how students would rate other schools: Wheaton College was "liberal" because students could attend movies; Moody Bible Institute was tilting dangerously because it allowed such vices as holding hands as long as they were practiced off campus. But we were still pure. We hadn't dropped our guard. We took a kind of perverse delight in how different we were.

2. *It breeds hypocrisy.* When rules are so clearly spelled out, it is easy to make the grade. Those who follow the rules soon relax in a sense of smug satisfaction, and it is easy to overlook hidden sins. Jesus said the Pharisees were like a cup that is clean on the outside and dirty on the inside. I could see the results of this in myself and my fellow students. We were too busy playing spiritual exercise games to show love and understanding to people who needed them.

And we were too busy measuring skirt lengths to worry about war or racism or world hunger.

3. *It is addictive.* Legalism can be just as much a power game as climbing the corporate ladder, or climbing the social ladder in high school or college. In my high school there was an unwritten game to see who could collect the longest list of school activities under their yearbook photo. The winners were rewarded with status and attention, a sense of power that they had beaten out all the rest. Jesus said that even spirituality can be misused like that.

Christians can flex their muscles at each other as a technique for pumping up their own egos, while they gradually grow callous toward others. The company vice-president who clawed his way to the top is likely to have little sympathy for the peons still beneath him: "I scrambled up the ladder; he can too." When someone in Bible college committed a blatant sin, the natural response was to judge and ostracize rather than to forgive.

4. *It lowers your view of God.* Legalists fool you. They are so dedicated, so obviously concerned with their faith that you would think they have a very high view of God. But the danger in legalism is that is lowers the sights. If my requirements as a Christian are spelled out in a rulebook, that is *all* I have to do. I can arrive. I can meet God's approval. The best legalists I knew felt secure and comfortable, like the Pharisees. They had fulfilled the law, had they not? But to those people Jesus shouts with a vengeance, "Fools!" No one ever *arrives* in the Christian life. We have to depend on God for the rest of our lives.

In summary, legalists miss the whole point of the gospel, that it is a gift freely given by God to people who don't deserve it. Legalists try to prove how much they deserve God's love. Assuredly, God is not impressed.

The rigid Old Testament law, Paul said, was like a schoolmaster to prove to us how far short of God we come. The law proves we cannot reach God, so God had to reach out to us, dying for us and restoring us to himself. Yet somehow legalists end up feeling more proud than grateful.

After studying Jesus' extensive treatment of the Pharisees in the two chapters I have mentioned, I tried to trace a common thread. I believe that all these characteristics are natural results of people who associate only with each other all day. The Pharisees were simply around other Pharisees too much. They began competing with one another. By trying to impress each other with their love for God, they lost contact with the real enemy: Satan and his grip on non-Christians.

Not an External Exercise

Is legalism only found in the Bible Belt? No, legalism is like the common cold: no one is exempt. It quickly spreads through any group. I know Christians who think themselves more spiritual and enlightened than others because they feel free to drink wine and smoke pipes. But they have the same legalist problems.

A meticulous researcher named Merton Strommen surveyed seven thousand Protestant church youth from many denominations, asking them whether they agreed with the following statements:

"The way to be accepted by God is to try sincerely to live a good life." More than 60 percent agreed.

"God is satisfied if a person lives the best life he can." Almost 70 percent agreed.

"The main emphasis of the gospel is on God's rules for right living." More than half agreed.

> **"A lot of people have made Christianity into a bunch of rules, questions, and answers. That way they avoid having to have a real relationship with God."**

If is as if the apostle Paul and Martin Luther had never opened their mouths! Christians still believe following a code of rules gets you to heaven!

This kind of thinking can prove fatal to a Christian's faith, and it may help explain a troubling phenomenon among Christians. I have known dozens of kids who grew up in wonderful Christian homes and sound churches but decided later to scrap their faith. After being outstanding examples of Christianity for a while, they become spiritual dropouts.

I have come to believe that many of them failed because they concentrated on the exterior, visible Christian life. When their Christian friends behaved a certain way and spoke a certain language, they began mimicking their behavior. They became walking mirrors, reflecting all the correct styles and patterns of the church. Though there was no content to their faith, they were so skilled at following the rules that no one noticed the inside. Faith as an external exercise is very easy to cast aside, as a snake sheds its skin. A person can discard a legalistic brand of Christianity just by trading it for a new set of rules, like those of Krishna Consciousness or Bahai or secular humanism.

If you develop Christian strength by focusing instead on the living Christ, it becomes much more difficult to shed.

A WORD CALLED GRACE

Jesus did not, of course, teach that holiness is unimportant. But he carefully avoided legalism. Several times people asked Jesus for advice on a specific problem. Usually he wouldn't give a specific interpretation of an Old Testament rule; instead, he pointed to the principle behind the rule. He didn't tell a rich person to give away 18.5 percent of his goods; he said give them all away. He didn't define adultery as actual sexual intercourse; instead, he condemned the principle of using women as sexual objects so that men commit adultery in their hearts. Love? That is not an easy thing to achieve even among friends. But Jesus says, "Love your enemies!" Murder? "I have added to that rule," Jesus says. "If you are merely angry, even in your own home, you are in danger of judgment!"

I could develop a list of rules stricter than those of any Bible college. But Jesus specialized in wiping out legalistic obligations by saying, "No, there is much more to it than that." He never replaces my goals with something easier. He replaces them with something impossible.

Not that Jesus doesn't care about how we live. He does care, and that is why he continues pointing out the lofty principles which should guide our lives. Jesus lashes out at legalism so that we will never pile up a list of credits on how good we are. The credit goes to God, not to us.

Christians use a word called "grace" that can be a cure for legalism. Grace simply means that God's love is freely given, with no strings attached. Grace is the exact opposite of legalism. Grace is what Jesus gave and gives. Grace is the gift of Jesus himself.

It is hard for me to accept gifts. I am used to achieving because I work at something. I get good grades or make the tennis team or sell an article only if I drive myself. So it is difficult for me to accept grace, too. I would rather *earn* God's favor. But because of grace, I don't have to go around trying to impress God with how spiritual I am. Grace helps me to relax, to trust God, to realize he is already impressed enough to call me "a gift that he delights in" (Ephesians 1:11 LB). This is what Josh reminded me of so forcefully. Grace means that God is not finished with us yet—we are rough and unruly and cantankerous, but he still treats us as though we are the most beautiful of all his creations.

Somehow Christians tend to forget about grace. We become *proud* of our faith because it solves some of our problems and sets us apart from other people. We forget that, as Josh said, the only consistent difference between us and the rest of the world is that we have admitted we are sinners. The only good in us is a result of God's free grace.

Paul said, "For he chose us in him before the creation of the world to be holy and blameless in his sight" (Ephesians 1:4).

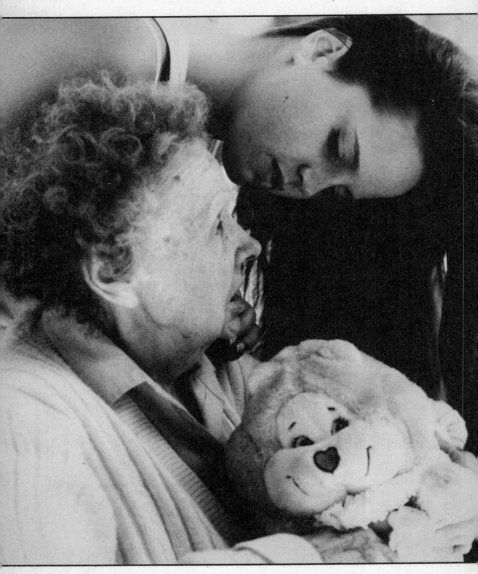

Fact #9

A LOVING GOD DOES SOMETIMES LET SUFFERING HAPPEN

But That's Not
His Final Word

By Philip Yancey

I once watched a television interview with a famous Hollywood actress whose lover drowned in a harbor near Los Angeles. The police investigation revealed he had rolled off a yacht in a drunken stupor. The actress looked at the camera, her beautiful features contorted with grief, and asked bizarrely, "How could a loving God let this happen?"

The actress probably had not thought about God for months. But suddenly, in the face of pain, she lashed out in anger against him. For her and for nearly everyone, doubt follows pain like a reflex action. We hurt, and instinctively we turn against God regardless of the circumstances. We can't help blaming him and then doubting him.

In two decades of writing I have interviewed many people in pain. Some of them, like one teenage pilot who ran out of fuel and crashed in a cornfield, were directly responsible for their own suffering. Others, like a young woman who died of leukemia six months after her wedding day, were seemingly struck at random with no warning. Yet all of them, without exception, experienced deep and nagging doubts about God because of the pain.

Pain calls our most basic beliefs about God into question. Over and over again I have heard four major questions brought on by pain: *Is God competent? Is he really so powerful? Is he fair? Why doesn't he seem to care about pain?* I know those questions well, for I have also asked them when I have suffered. If you have not yet asked them yourself, you probably will someday, when severe pain strikes.

IS GOD COMPETENT?

When phrased that boldly, the question sounds strange and even heretical. But I believe many of our questions about pain trace back to the issue of God's competence. Does he know what he's doing? He created the whole world we live in. Couldn't he have done a slightly better job?

The world abounds with beauty, to be sure. Merely take a walk in a garden in the springtime, or watch snow fall on a mountain landscape, and for a moment all seems right with the world. Doubts vanish. The world reflects God's greatness as a painting reflects the genius of an artist.

But look closer at this lovely world and you begin to notice pain and suffering everywhere. Animals devour each other in a vicious food cycle. People destroy one another. And everything that lives eventually dies. God's "painting" appears flawed, ruined.

I confess that I once viewed pain as God's one great goof in an otherwise impressive world. Why would he mess up such a world by including pain in it? Without pain and suffering, we would find it so much easier to respect and trust him. Why didn't he simply create all the beautiful things in the world, but leave out pain?

I lost my doubts about God's competence in a very unusual place. To my amazement I found that a world without pain actually exists within the walls of a leprosy hospital. As I walked the corridors of a leprosarium in Louisiana and got to know victims of the disease, my doubts faded away.

People with leprosy do not feel physical pain—that, in fact, is the peculiar tragedy of their disease. As the disease spreads, nerve endings that carry pain signals fall silent. Thus, leprosy patients offer a window into what a painless world would look like.

Nobody I know envies the life of a leprosy victim. People normally respond to the disease with fear and revulsion. Why? Because of our visual images (often distorted through sensational novels and movies) of the disease. It is a cruel dieseease, and untreated it can cause gross deformity on the hands and feet and face. I know of no lonelier people in the world than leprosy victims.

But here is the most astounding fact about leprosy, a fact that went undiscovered until the 1950s. Virtually all the physical deformity comes about *because the leprosy victim cannot feel pain*. The disease destroys only pain cells; all other tissue damage is caused by the patient's inability to sense pain.

I met a leprosy patient who lost all the toes on his right foot simply because he insisted on wearing tight and narrow shoes. I know another who nearly lost his thumb because of a sore that developed when he gripped a mop handle too hard. Scores of patients at that hospital have gone blind merely because leprosy silenced the pain cells designed to alert them when to blink. Over time, without blinking, their eyes dried out.

"Where is God's love in this much pain? If this is his will for me, then I'm not so sure I want to follow it."

I learned that in a thousand ways large and small, pain serves us each day. If we are healthy, pain cells alert us when to change shoes, when to loosen our grip on a mop handle or rake, when to blink. In short, pain allows us to lead a free and active life. If you ever doubt that, visit a leprosarium and observe for yourself a world without pain.

My research into the nature of pain impressed me so much that eventually I wrote a book (*Where Is God When It Hurts?*) that describes some of the remarkable features of the pain network in our bodies. I cannot reproduce them all here, but a few are worth mentioning:

- Without pain's warnings, most sports would be far too risky.
- Without pain, there would be no sex, for sexual pleasure is mostly carried by pain cells.
- Without pain, art and culture would be very limited.
- Musicians, dancers, painters, and sculptors all rely on the body's sensitivity to pain and pressure. A guitarist, for example must be able to feel exactly where his finger lands on the string and how hard it presses.
- Without pain, our lives would be in constant mortal danger.

Those rare people who feel no pain have no warning of a ruptured appendix, heart attack, or brain tumor. Most of them die young because of some medical problem that went undetected due to their insensitivity to pain.

I came away from my research into pain with a bedrock conviction that pain is essential to normal life on this planet. It is not an innovation God devised at the last moment of creation just to make our lives miserable. Nor is it his one great goof. That doubt has now vanished. I now look at the incredible network of millions of pain sensors all over our bodies, precisely gauged to our need for protection, and see an example of God's competence, not incompetence.

IS GOD POWERFUL?

Of course physical pain is only the top layer of what we call suffering. Death, diseases, earthquakes, tornadoes—all of these summon up harder questions about God's involvement on earth. It is one thing to say he originally designed the pain system as an effective warning for us. But what about the world now?

Can God possibly be satisfied with all the rampant human evil and natural disasters and child-killing diseases? Why doesn't he step in with all his competence and put an end to some of the worst kinds of suffering? Is he powerful enough? Does he have the ability to rearrange the universe in a way that would relieve our suffering?

Not long ago a surprising book on this very topic edged up on the best-seller charts. It was a book about theology by a rabbi, and it dealt with an unpleasant subject, the problem of pain. The book: *When Bad Things Happen to Good People*, by Rabbi Harold Kushner.

Kushner's doubts about God began to surface when his infant son was diagnosed with the disease progeria. Somehow, no one knows how, progeria wildly speeds up the process of aging. Instead of growing, a child with progeria starts shrinking just like a very old person. Kushner's son went bald. His skin turned leathery and wrinkled. Teeth that had only recently appeared started falling out. By the calendar the boy was barely school age, but he had the body of an old man. Eventually, at the age of eight, he died.

During the agonizing process of his son's disease, Harold Kushner still served as a rabbi. He had to go to widows and widowers, to people in hospitals, to other parents of suffering children, and represent God to them. He found that he could no longer believe some things about God.

A famous philosopher once posed the problem of pain this way: "Either God is all-powerful or he is all-loving. He cannot be both and allow pain and suffering." Ultimately, Kushner concluded that he too could no longer believe in an all-powerful, all-loving God.

In his book, Kushner explains that he came to accept God's love, but began to question God's power. He now believes that God is good, and loves us, and hates to see us suffer. Unfortunately, God's hands are tied. He simply isn't powerful enough to straighten out the problems of this world—problems like children with the disease progeria.

Kushner's book became a best-seller because people found it

comforting. They felt relieved. Kushner had voiced for them what they had wanted to believe all along: that God desired to help but could not. When we call on him to solve our problems, we are simply expecting too much of God.

I also found much comfort in Rabbi Kushner's book—so much that it began to trouble me. His ideas sound like something I may want to be true. But are they true? My problems grew larger as I studied the book in light of the Bible, a book given by God to tell us about himself and the nature of this world.

In one chapter, Kushner cites the book of Job, and I turned to the Old Testament book about a man who suffered great, undeserved pain. God delivered a speech to Job and his three friends after they had spent many long days thrashing over the problem of pain. If anyone deserved an answer to the problem of pain, it was Job. He, the most righteous man in the world, had suffered the most.

But the speech Job got (chapters 38–41) was not at all what he expected. No apologies from God. No "Sorry, friend, but I had other things on my mind." No real explanation of the problem of pain. Mainly, Job got a lesson in running the universe.

"Brace yourself like a man," God began. "I will question you, and you shall answer me." Then God launched into a tour of the cosmos.

> *"Where were you when I laid the earth's*
> *foundation?*
> *Tell me, if you understand.*
> *Who marked off its dimensions?*
> *Surely you know!"*
>
> (38:4–5)

Step by step, God led Job through the process of creation: designing the planet earth, carving out troughs for the sea, setting the solar system into motion, working out the crystalline structure of snowflakes. Then he turned to animals, pointing with pride to a mountain goat and the wild ox and ostrich and horse and hawk.

"Will the one who contends with the Almighty correct him?" God asked in conclusion (40:2). "Let him who accuses God answer him!"

Novelist Frederick Buechner summed up the confrontation in Job this way: "God doesn't explain. He explodes. He asks Job who he thinks he is anyway. He says that to try to explain the kind of things Job wants explained would be like trying to explain Einstein to a little-neck clam . . . God doesn't reveal his grand design. He reveals himself."

With Job, God had a perfect platform to discuss his lack of power, if that indeed was the problem. Surely Job would have welcomed these words from God: "Job, I'm truly sorry about what's happening. I hope you realize I had nothing to do with the way things turned out. I wish I could help, Job, but I really can't."

God said no such thing. Speaking to a wounded, thoroughly demoralized man, he celebrated his own wisdom and power. If that is true— and you can read it for yourself in Job 38–41—I must question Rabbi Kushner's theory about God's powerlessness. Why did God choose the worst possible situation, when his power was most called to question, to talk about his power?

> **"I always thought my faith in God could get me through anything. But it's hard to talk to him when you hurt so much you can't even think straight."**

Other parts of the Bible convince me that perhaps we ought to view the problem of pain as a matter of timing, not of power. We get plenty of indication that God is unsatisfied with the state of this world, surely as unsatisfied as we are. He doesn't like the violence, the warfare, the hatred, the suffering. And he plans to do something about it one day.

All through the prophets and through Jesus' life and the New Testament runs a theme of hope, of a great day when a new heaven and new earth will be fashioned to replace the old. The apostle Paul puts it this way, "I consider that our present sufferings are not worth comparing with the glory that will be revealed in us. The creation waits in eager expectation for the sons of God to be revealed. . . . We know that the whole creation has been groaning as in the pains of childbirth right up to the present time" (Romans 8:18, 19, 22).

At times, living in the "groaning" creation, we cannot help feeling like poor old Job, who scratched his sores with shards of pottery and wondered why God was allowing him to suffer. Like Job, we are called to trust God, even when all the evidence seems stacked against him. We are asked to believe that he does control the universe and does have ultimate power, regardless of how things may appear.

And we must not make the mistake of judging God by the state of the world now. He plans a much better world someday, a world without pain or evil or tears or death. He asks for our trust in him and in his power to bring about that new creation.

IS GOD FAIR?

"Why me?" we ask almost instinctively when we face great tragedy. *Two thousand cars were driving in the rain on the expressway—why did mine skid into a bridge? Lift lines were crowded with skiers all day—why was I the one to break a leg and ruin my vacation? A rare type of cancer strikes only one in a hundred people—why did my father have to be among the victims?*

Look at those questions carefully and you can detect a common thread. Each questioner assumes that God was somehow responsible, that he directly caused the pain. If, in fact, he is all-competent and all-powerful, then doesn't that mean he controls every detail of life?

Did God hand-select which car would fishtail across the highway? Did he direct one skier, but not others, to slalom over a hidden stump? Does he choose cancer victims at random out of a telephone book?

Few of us can avoid such thoughts when pain hits us. Immediately we begin to search our consciences for some sin that God must be punishing: What is God trying to tell me through my pain? And if we find nothing definite, we begin to question God's fairness: Why am I suffering more than my neighbor, who is an outright jerk?

The suffering people I have interviewed torment themselves with such questions. As they writhe in bed, they wonder about God. Often, well-meaning Christians only make them feel worse. They come to the hospital room bearing gifts of guilt ("You must have done something to deserve this") and frustration ("You must not be praying hard enough").

Once again, the only place to truly test out our doubts about God is the Bible. What do we find there—does God ever use pain as punishment? Yes, he does. The Bible records many examples, especially punishment directed against the Old Testament nation of Israel. But notice: In every case, punishment follows repeated warnings against the behavior that merits the punishment. The books of the Old Testament prophets, hundreds of pages long, give a loud and eloquent warning to Israel to turn from sin before judgment.

Think of a parent who punishes a young child. It would do little good for that parent to sneak up at odd times during a day and whap the child without any explanation. Such tactics would produce a neurotic, not an obedient, child. Effective punishment must be clearly related to behavior.

The nation of Israel knew why they were being punished; the prophets had warned them in excruciating detail. The Pharaoh of Egypt knew exactly why the ten plagues were unleashed against his land: God had predicted them and told him why they would happen and how a change of heart could prevent them.

Biblical examples of suffering-as-punishment, then, tend to fit a pattern. The pain comes after much warning, and no one sits around afterward asking, "Why?" They know very well why they are suffering.

But does that pattern resemble what happens to most of us today? Do we get a direct revelation from God warning us of a coming catastrophe? Does personal suffering come packaged with a clear explanation from God? If not, I have to question whether the pains most of us feel—a skiing accident, cancer in the family, a traffic mishap—really are punishments from God.

Frankly, I believe that unless God specially reveals otherwise, we would be best to look to other biblical examples of people who suffered. And the Bible contains some stories of people who suffered but definitely were not being punished by God.

Once again, Job provides the very best example. He, too, questioned God's fairness, with good reason: God himself described Job as "blameless and upright, a man who fears God and shuns evil" (1:8). Why, then, must he endure such an ordeal?

Job's friends insisted the problem was with Job, not God. After all, they reasoned, God is fair and does not make mistakes. Job, despite his protests of innocence, must have done something to deserve his pain.

Thousands of years have passed, but we keep falling back on the same explanations of suffering that Job's friends voiced. We forget that those explanations were dismissed with a scowl by God at the end of the book. God insisted that Job had done nothing at all to deserve his pain. It was not a punishment for his behavior.

Jesus made the same point in two different places in the New Testament. Once, his disciples pointed to a blind man and asked who had sinned to bring on such suffering—the blind man or his parents. Jesus replied that neither one had sinned (John 9:1–5). Another time, Jesus commented on two current events from his day: The collapse of a tower that killed eighteen people and a government-ordered slaughter of some worshipers in the temple. Those people, said Jesus, were no guiltier than anyone else (Luke 13:1–5). They too had done nothing to deserve their pain.

I have concluded that most Christians who suffer today are not being punished by God. Rather, their suffering fits the pattern of unexpected, unexplained pain such as that described by Job and the victims of the catastrophes Jesus described.

There are exceptions, of course. Some pain does have a clear connection to behavior: victims of drug addiction and venereal disease don't need to waste time trying to figure out the "message" of their pain. But for most of us, most of the time, I see no easy explanation for pain in the Bible.

Why did Job suffer? Why did the man have to endure blindness? Why did those people get trapped in a falling tower? To such questions the Bible gives no neat answer. We live in an imperfect world, and not everything works out the way we wish. If anything, the book of Job implies that the answer is beyond human understanding. To figure out why everything in this world works the way it does is about like a little-neck clam trying to comprehend Einstein.

Consistently, the Bible directs the issue away from a question of cause to a question of response, "Is God fair?" we ask in the midst of our pain. "I am in control, no matter how it looks," is his only answer. And then he has a question for us, one question: "Do you trust me?"

DOES GOD CARE?

The last great doubt that arises in the midst of pain is subtly different. Other questions are more abstract, philosophical. This one is personal. Why doesn't God show more concern for us in a time of need? If he cares about my pain, why doesn't he let me know it?

A great Christian author named C. S. Lewis wrote a classic book on pain called simply *The Problem of Pain*. In it he answered convincingly many of the doubts that spring up when Christians suffer. Hundreds of thousands of people have found comfort in Lewis's book.

But years after Lewis wrote the book, his wife contracted cancer. He watched her wither away in a hospital bed, and then watched her die. After her death, he wrote another book on pain, this one far more personal and emotional. And in that book, *A Grief Observed*, C.S. Lewis says this:

> *Meanwhile, where is God? This is one of the most dis-*
> *quieting symptoms. When you are happy, so happy that*
> *you have no sense of needing him, if you turn to him*
> *then with praise, you will be welcomed with open arms.*
> *But go to him when your need is desperate, when all*
> *other help is vain and what do you find? A door slammed*
> *in your face, and a sound of bolting and double bolting*
> *on the inside. After that, silence. You may as well turn*
> *away.*

C.S. Lewis did not question the existence of God, but he did question God's love. At no time had God seemed more distant or unconcerned. Did God really love? If so, where was he at such a time of grief? Not everyone feels the sense of abandonment described by C.S. Lewis. Some Christians express that God became particularly real to them in their time of grief. He can offer a mysterious comfort that helps transcend the pain we are feeling. But not always. Sometimes he seems utterly silent. What then? Does God care only for people who somehow *feel* his comfort?

I have talked to enough people in pain to realize that experiences differ. I cannot generalize about how many individuals will experience the closeness or distance of God. But there are two expressions of God's concern that apply to all of us everywhere. One is the response of Jesus to pain. And the other involves everyone who calls himself a Christian.

Even the most faithful Christians may, like C.S. Lewis, question God's personal concern. At such a time, prayers seem like words hurled into the void. Few of us get a miraculous appearance of a loving God to calm our doubts. But at least we have this: An actual glimpse of how God truly feels about pain.

In Jesus we have the historical fact of how God responded to pain on earth, and anyone who doubts· God's love should take another look at him. He gives the up-close and personal side of God's response to human suffering. All our doubts about God and suffering should, in fact, be filtered through what we know about Jesus.

First there is the amazing fact that God himself took on pain. The same God who boasted to Job of his power in creating the world chose to subject himself to that world and all of its natural laws, including pain. Another Christian writer, Dorothy Sayers, put it this way:

> *For whatever reason God chose to make man as he is— limited and suffering and subject to sorrows and death— he had the honesty and courage to take his own medicine. Whatever game he is playing with his creation, he has kept his own rules and played fair. He can exact nothing from man that he has not exacted from himself. He has himself gone through the whole of human experience, from the trivial irritations of family life and the cramping re- strictions of hard work and lack of money to the worst horrors of pain and humiliation, defeat, despair, and death. When he was a man, he played the man. He was born in poverty and died in disgrace and thought it well worthwhile.*

"For God so loved the world," says the Bible's most familiar verse, "that he gave his one and only Son, that whoever believes in him shall not perish but have eternal life" (John 3:16). The fact that Jesus came and suffered and died does not remove pain from our lives. Nor does it guarantee that we will always feel comforted. But it does show that God did not sit idly by and watch us suffer alone.

He joined us and in his life on earth endured far more pain than most of us ever will. In doing so, he won a victory that will make possible a future world without pain.

The word "compassion" comes from two Latin words that mean "to suffer with." Jesus showed compassion in the deepest sense when he voluntarily came to earth and took on pain. He suffered with us, and for us.

Jesus spent much of his life among suffering people, and his response to them also shows us how God feels about pain. When Jesus' friend died, he wept. Very often—and every time he was directly asked—he healed the pain.

How does God feel about our pain? Look at Jesus. He responded to hurting people with sadness and grief. And then he reached out with supernatural power and healed the causes of pain. I doubt that Jesus' disciples tormented themselves with questions like "Does God care?" They had visible evidence of his concern every day. They simply looked at Jesus' face and watched him as he performed God's mission on earth.

But Jesus did not stay on earth. Today we cannot fly to Jerusalem, rent a car, and schedule a personal appointment with him. What about those of us today? How can we sense God's love? We have the Holy Spirit, of course, an actual sign of God's presence in us. And we have the promise of the future when God will set the world right and meet us face to face. But what about right now? What can reassure us physically and visibly of God's love on earth?

That is where the church comes in, the community that includes every person on earth who truly follows God. The Bible uses the phrase "the body of Christ," and that phrase expresses what we are to be about. We are called to represent what Christ is like, especially to those in pain.

The apostle Paul must have had something like that process in mind when he wrote these words: "[God] comforts us in all our troubles, so that we can comfort those in any trouble with the comfort we ourselves have received from God. For just as the sufferings of Christ flow over into our lives, so also through Christ our comfort overflows" (2 Corinthians 1:3–5).

There is only one good way to understand how the body of Christ can minister to a suffering person, and that is to see it in action. I have seen it, and I will end this chapter by telling you about Martha, a person who lived with great pain and great doubts.

Martha was a very attractive twenty-six-year-old woman when I first met her. Her life was permanently changed one day when she learned she had contracted ALS, or Lou Gehrig's disease. ALS destroys nerve control. It first attacks voluntary movements, such as control over arms and legs, then hands and feet. It progresses on to involuntary movements, finally affecting breathing and causing death. Sometimes a person's body succumbs quickly, sometimes not.

Martha seemed perfectly normal when she first told me about her illness. But a month later she was using a wheelchair. She got fired from her job at a university library. Within another month, Martha had lost use of her right arm. Soon she lost use of both arms and could barely move the hand controls on a new electric wheelchair.

I began visiting Martha at her rehabilitation hospital. I took her for short rides in her wheelchair and in my car. I learned about the indignity of her suffering. She needed help with every move: getting dressed, arranging her head on the pillow, cleaning her bedpan. When she cried, someone else had to wipe her tears and hold a tissue to her nose. Her body was in utter revolt against her will. It would not obey any of her commands.

We talked about death and briefly about the Christian faith. I confess to you readily that the great Christian hopes of eternal life, ultimate healing, and resurrection sounded hollow and frail and thin as smoke when held up to someone like Martha. She wanted no angel wings, but an arm that did not flop to the side, a mouth that did not drool, and lungs that would not collapse on her. I confess that eternity, even a pain-free eternity, seemed to have a strange irrelevance to the suffering Martha felt.

She thought about God, of course, but she could hardly think of him with love. She held out against any deathbed conversion, insisting that, as she put it, she would only turn to God out of love and not out of fear. And how could she love a God who let her suffer so?

It became clear around October that ALS would complete its horrible cycle quickly in Martha. She had great difficulty breathing. Because of reduced oxygen supply to her brain, she tended to fall asleep in the middle of conversations. Sometimes at night she would awake in a panic with a sensation like choking and be unable to call for help.

Martha badly wanted at least two weeks out of the hospital, in her own apartment in Chicago, as a time to invite friends over one by one in order to say good-bye and to come to terms with her death. But the two weeks in her apartment posed a problem. How could she get the round-the-clock care she needed? Some government aid could be found to keep her in a hospital room, but not at home, not with the intensive care she needed just to stay alive.

Only one group in all of Chicago offered the free and loving personal care that Martha needed: The Reba Place Fellowship of Evanston. That Christian community adopted Martha as a project and volunteered all that was necessary to fulfill her last wishes. Sixteen women rearranged their lives for her. They divided into work teams, traded off baby-sitting duties for their own children, and moved in. They stayed with Martha, listened to her ravings and complaints, bathed her, helped her sit up, moved her, stayed up with her all night, prayed for her, and loved her. They were available. They gave her time and gave meaning to her suffering. To Martha they became God's body.

The Reba Place women also explained to Martha the Christian hope. And finally after seeing the love of God enfleshed in his body, the people around her—although to her God himself seemed uncompassionate, even cruel—Martha came to that God in Christ and presented herself in trust to the one who had died for her. She did not come to God in fear; she had found his love at last. On the faces of the women of Reba Place Fellowship she was able to read the love of God. In a very moving service in Evanston, she feebly gave a testimony and was baptized.

On the day before Thanksgiving of 1983 Martha died. Her

body, crumpled and misshapen, was a pathetic imitation of its former beauty. When it finally stopped functioning, Martha left it.

But today Martha lives, in a new body, in wholeness and triumph. She lives because of the victory that Christ won and because of his body, the church, who made that victory known to her. She met God through her suffering, for it was during that time of suffering that she learned what he was truly like. In the love and compassion of the Christians around her, she saw the love and compassion of God himself. And her doubts about him gradually fell away.

MICHAEL SILUK

Fact #10

YOU WILL HAVE TO OBEY SOME RULES THAT GO AGAINST YOUR GRAIN

*But Discipline
Results in
Greater Strength*

by Tim Stafford

For many new Christians, relating to God is fine as long as what they get from God is love and forgiveness. But then they go to church and find that some of the things they like to do are frowned on. They start reading the Bible and are confronted with orders on what to do with money, family, time, and any number of things. They find that they are not supposed to get drunk, they are supposed to wait until marriage for sex, and in the meantime they are supposed to obey their parents. Those are the written rules. The orders do not even stop there. In praying to God, new Christians get the definite, uncomfortable impression God wants to change them.

At this point—and at many, many points thereafter—Christians face a decision. Will they obey? Or will they avoid the issue? Not too many actually say out loud, "I don't want to obey those rules. I prefer to run my own life. What I do with my boyfriend/girlfriend is my business. I have chosen my friends, and they are the most important thing to me. I am the way I am because I like being myself. If God wants to change me, he'll have to catch me."

Many, however, silently make a decision that amounts to saying that. They keep on doing what they want to do. And gradually, almost invisibly, their faith fades away. They may continue Christian activity. But it's just on the surface. When they start college, or go to a new town, or get very busy with work, they often drop out entirely. People want to know, then, "What happened?" In reality, what happened took place long before.

We who resent interference from parents or neighbors naturally don't want God's interference either. This is a major reason why some people never listen to God. They think of the Bible as a two-thousand-page extension of the Ten Commandments, and they shut their minds to it.

Actually, the Bible has relatively few commandments. For every rule there are pages of poetry, history, biography, or theology. But there is no getting around the fact that God has advice to give us on dozens of subjects, and he conveys it in the most authoritative way possible. He says, "Do this or you will die." How dogmatic can you get? A lot of people in our individualistic world can't begin to imagine submitting themselves to that kind of unyielding authority. And why should they? Does it really make sense to surrender your autonomy to someone you can't see and don't even know very well?

I recognize this as a serious objection because I share the problem. I like what God says so long as it agrees with me. Unfortunately, it doesn't always.

My problem with the rules in the Bible boils down to one simple fact: I don't like to be told what to do. I have loads of advice to share with others, of course. I would be happy to advise you on everything from the best way to brush your teeth to the opinion you ought to have held on the movie you liked. But I stiffen the moment someone else tries to advise me.

I noticed this problem on a Sierra Nevada backpacking trip. Three of my companions were just as opinionated as I was. We had an unusually fine week of hiking, but it included a lot of bickering. If I selected a spot under the trees that would make a wonderful place to spend the night, Greg would quickly point out that we would not get much morning sun there; Steve would observe that it was far from the water; and Dave would say that we really ought to hike a few more miles before stopping.

Once we had set up camp, each of us seemed to know exactly how much work he had done. If Dave suggested that it was Greg's turn to wash the dishes, Greg would quickly point out that he had already gathered firewood and started the fire. Any subject that came up—where to camp, what to cook, which way to hike— brought forth several confident opinions. I didn't think much about it. That's just the way it is when you hike with people like me. We love to give advice, and we hate to take it.

But a few days into the trip, camped beside a small ice-blue lake cradled in the arms of a high granite mountain, I began to notice some-thing odd about Mark. He didn't fit. While the rest of us busily gave advice and formulated flawless argu-ments to prove how right we were, Mark had little to say. When he did make a suggestion, he made it quiet-ly. Strangely, though, his sugges-tions were not followed by the sound of four jaws clicking into action with other opinions. He was met by silence or the rustle of people mov-ing to do what he had suggested. Mark seemed to have a mysterious power: He could make us want to respond to what he said.

> **"Parents, teachers, coaches, cops— everyone is always telling me what to do. Why does God have to order me around as well?"**

I thought long and hard, pondering what his power might be. It finally came to me. We responded to Mark without resentment because of the kind of person we knew he was. For one thing, he didn't give advice for the pleasure of feeling his tongue move. He thought about what he was going to say before he said it, and his suggestions were almost always wise. Why waste time discussing other options? Mark could be trusted to give good advice. When he spoke, he seemed to have already thought through the situation.

Of course, good advice is not always pleasant to hear. It is not fun to resume a standing position on feet tired from hiking all day so that you can set up a tent. No one leaps to wash the dishes in a freezing stream long after the sun has gone to bed. Yet somehow even Mark's unpleasant suggestions were easier to follow. That was because we knew that Mark would never suggest some job he wouldn't do himself. He simply never tried to get out of work. If a job turned out to be harder than we had anticipated, he would pitch in and help. He never left us stranded doing our "fair share" while he loafed around the campfire.

CONSIDER THE SOURCE

God's advice, like Mark's, is easier to take if you understand the kind of person God is. For one thing, his advice is not arbitrary. We listened to Mark because he was thoughtful and wise didn't just toss up arbitrary opinions. If that made it easier to listen to Mark, why not God? He made the world we live in. He made you. No one understands your circumstances better than he does. If you can get his advice, why insist on figuring out everything for yourself?

I've thought about this particularly in regard to sex. A person can make a pretty good argument against God's view of sex. Logically, I can't defeat a person who wants to believe that sex is pleasant and harmless fun. Especially in the first decades after the pill was invented, a lot of very smart people became convinced that restricting your sex life to one partner was as outmoded as using a buggy whip to drive your car. Experience, however, has shown that God's view had more wisdom than we could see. After a generation of AIDS, herpes, two million American abortions per year, uncountable broken families, and expanding loneliness and sexual frustration, I feel considerably more secure in asserting, "Even when I don't understand God's view, I'd better listen."

And then, Mark was easier to listen to because he would never dodge the dirtiest job. God doesn't either. It would be hard to take advice from a God who sat in heaven, shielded from the terrible temptation and frustrations and suffering that can go along with being a human being. You can almost hear the protesting sneers, "He gives good advice, but can he take it himself?" The answer is that he can. God has not dodged the dirtiest job: In Jesus he came to face all our temptations and to die the cruelest death possible. Yet he took his own advice exactly and lived a perfect life. He doesn't demand of you what he would not or could not do himself.

You cannot get around the fact, though, that God's advice is terribly hard. He says, for instance, that I am supposed to love my neighbor the same way I love myself, forgive my brother endlessly, and never worry about where my next paycheck is coming from. Maybe Jesus could do it, but I cannot.

What makes the difference is this: Like Mark, God does not hand me the list of chores and leave me to do them alone. He helps me. More than Mark (because God is much more powerful), God will make it possible for me to do them. Without his help his commandments are impossible. Relying on him, I can begin to live as I should.

So his commandments can be read, not as harsh demands, but as promises. He says, "Don't worry about money." But the unwritten clause is, "I will provide for your needs. I will make it possible for you to relax and trust me."

This does not mean that I am utterly delighted when I get advice from God. I am a stubborn person: I like to have things my way, without listening to anyone. But I have come to see that some people's advice is worth taking.

What About Ungodly Authorities?

There is another problem that I have run into in my Christian life. Advice sometimes comes from ungodlike people—my parents, my teachers, my colleagues, or my boss. It is one thing to take advice from God and quite another to take it from these faulty, frequently uptight people. Suppose a father has a bad day and demands that his son call off a date to help around the house—should the son obey such an unreasonable demand?

Yet there are verses scattered through the Bible that make a parent's authority quite clear. "Children, obey your parents" (Colossians 3:20). God also requires allegiance to other authorities: "Everyone must submit himself to the governing authorities, for there is no authority except that which God has established" (Romans 13:1). God is a sensitive, all-knowing, helpful advice-giver. The authorities are different: They sometimes know nothing of what they are talking about and give orders only to prove that they can make you do what they want. Why should you bow to the chip on their shoulders? Why take advice when you know it is not the best?

Before I answer that, I would like to make it clear exactly what orders we are talking about. We are to respond to the people who have been put in authority over us *while* they are in authority over us. A student obeys a teacher while he is at school, not because that person is an adult or even because he is a teacher, but because teachers are in charge at school. If a teacher tells a student to do something after school is over, the student does not have to obey. The student should respect his teacher after school, as he ought to respect everyone. But he is not under obligation to obey.

The same goes for bosses. While you are working for them, you obey. Should you quit, you don't have to obey at all. A boss is not superior to you or even necessarily smarter or more knowledgeable. He is just the boss. Someone has to be.

This is even true of parents. Some people stretch the Scriptures to say you should always, all your life, obey your parents. The Bible doesn't say that. It says, "*Children*, obey your parents." It tells everyone of all ages to respect and honor parents, but only children are commanded to obey. I take that to mean that as long as you are under their roof and living off their livelihood, you obey. But when the time comes for you to establish a life of your own, you are not responsible to do what they say.

Are Authorities Even Necessary?

But why obey at all? I can think of four good reasons.

1. *In obeying authorities, you are obeying God.* God is the kind of advice-giver who makes advice easy to swallow. Here is one more piece of his advice: Obey those in authority over you. Just remember that you are not obeying them because of how wonderful they are, but because God asks you to. You are deferring to his authority, not theirs. He is not asking you to do something that he was unwilling to do himself. (Jesus toed the line even though it meant the authorities killed him unjustly.)

2. *Someone has to give orders, or we would live in chaos.* Some of the time you will know more than the person giving you orders. But you can't hold parliamentary debate every time a decision has to be made. Someone has to decide, even if he decides wrong. Very often it is more important to move than to move in a way that is 100 percent correct.

A teacher has to keep tabs on a whole classroom, not just on you. A parent has to think of the far-reaching consequences of a decision for every member of the family. A boss's job is to make sure everyone's work fits together. He may slight your work along the way, but I hope he has a better sense than you do of how your work relates to everyone else's. You may fry hamburgers better than anybody who ever lived, but if you are putting out more than the guys who wrap them can handle, it's your boss's job to slow you down.

> **"What makes God's commands so special anyway? Why should I bother obeying them? Does it really make any difference?"**

Now a boss or a parent or a teacher may fail to do a good job at coordinating everything. But how is he going to learn except by trying? If you insist on anarchy, things will never improve.

3. *Everyone is under authority part of the time.* Authority is what makes things happen; it is the "clutch" of the driveshaft, and without it action would never get from the engine to the wheels. When you go to a restaurant, you are under the "authority" of the waitress. She gets the agenda, tells you where to sit, takes your money from you. If you tried to get up and get your order for yourself, she would tell you to sit down. She would be right. Everyone has to learn to take orders—from a waitress or a teacher, from a store clerk or a traffic cop, or from the Internal Revenue Service.

4. *Authority usually protects a system that is worth saving.* I do not say obedience is easy. Sometimes you are placed under the authority of someone who really grates. You can't respect the person, so what do you do? In the army, where authority is absolute, there is a saying: "If you can't salute the man, salute the uniform." You don't have to respect the person, but you should respect enough the position he holds not to tear it down. Someday you may be promoted to the same position. You'd better hope that it still has some authority—that you don't have to "prove" every decision you make.

Take the family as an example. I can't think of anything more crucial to our world than good families. If you don't think so, find some people who come from bad families or no family at all. They tend to have problems all their lives.

But suppose your father can really act like a tyrant. In the years before you grow up and leave for good, you have two choices. You can defy him, fight him every step of the way, and correct every bad judgment he makes. As a result you probably won't have to do nearly so many unpleasant things. On the other hand, your "family" will hardly be a family anymore. You will survive, but your family will not. You will merely be a collection of people living under one roof.

The other option is to take literally Christ's advice that you "love your enemies"—in this case, your father. You decide to respect your father, not because he has earned respect, but because he is your father. Not only do you obey him, but you even try to act toward him as though he were really a good father. You ask his advice, get his opinion, and try to take him off the defensive. You salute the uniform, not the man; you treat him as the father he is not. You will survive—obedience will not kill you. Your family will survive, too. And the prospects are good that your father, once he is off the defensive, will loosen up somewhat.

We too easily get used to problems. We can act as though troubled families are just normal; the best anybody can do is survive. We can look at divorce statistics and say, "Marriage just doesn't work." We can look at the number of bad parents there are and say, "Family structures just don't work." But that is not quite accurate. They do not work easily—but they *can* work. With God's help, we can start turning back the tide of selfishness and sinfulness that makes authority so hard to live under. But if we give up on marriage or give up on families, we will have no raw material to work on. I think families matter enough to make "saluting the uniform" a worthwhile investment.

OVERCOMING FEARS ABOUT OBEDIENCE

People have two major concerns about taking advice. First, they worry about obeying something that is really wrong. After all, weren't Hitler's deputies just obeying orders when they murdered innocent Jews? Shouldn't they have thought for themselves?

Yes, they should have. But here is an important distinction: They ought to have thought for themselves, but not *by* themselves. They did not have to judge Hitler's orders by their own opinions. They could judge his orders—and his authority—by a clear standard God had given. God never sets up an authority—a parent, a ruler, a teacher, a boss—and says, "Do anything you want." He puts strict limits on authority. When Hitler stepped beyond the authority God had given him, Christians should have disobeyed.

There may be times in your life when someone, such as an employer, asks you to do something the Bible clearly says is wrong.

It is your responsibility to oppose him and to encourage him to return to the kind of authority God has given him. You are not saying. "You're such a lousy boss that I'm now going to take over your job," but rather "I want you, if possible, to become the kind of authority God wants you to be."

In the New Testament, the government was always respected. But when the government crossed over the line, refusing to allow Christians to tell about Jesus, Christians simply said, "That is not your right. You are in contradiction to God. Our first loyalty is to him."

The second worry people have is that, through obeying, one becomes a worm. This raises a serious question for me, because many people come out of their homes, schools, or jobs with personalities mashed into the color and consistency of oatmeal. God is not asking for this. He is not looking for someone who can't think for himself, who has no independence or spunk.

But authority does not, I believe, necessarily produce worms. In fact, I would guess that most people with strong, independent personalities developed their traits through the example of some strong, independent person who once had responsibility over them—perhaps a forceful mother or a dynamic teacher. I would guess that most worms are produced, not by strong authority, but by a confused, unloving situation. When chaos reigns in a family, a school, or a job, and people get lost in the cracks, they can be robbed of the full personality God wants for them. Authority and discipline do not, in themselves, destroy personality.

Read the Bible. Powerful personalities blaze through its pages—men and women whose lives changed history, who were afraid of nothing. Each model in the Bible is startlingly different, except for one similarity: They obeyed God. They lived under his authority. As a result, their strong personalities were strengthened, not weakened.

The Bible's model of obedience is a soldier trained for action. He is a strong person who has learned to work in the framework of an army, to accomplish things that could not otherwise be accomplished. That is the story of your life, if you are a Christian.

You must first be strong. And God lives in you, as a Christian, in order to make you strong. But then you are to harness that strength, being obedient to God's authority and working within the structures of families, jobs, government, and schools to focus that strength for some powerful good—to make a good family, to make a good school, to create a good place to work. You are not working for yourself. You are working for God. His advice is always worth taking.

GAIL DENHAM

Fact #11

IT'S HARD TO KEEP BELIEVING IN SOMETHING YOU CAN'T SEE

But It's Tougher to Believe in a World without Jesus

by Tim Stafford

I've met some weird Christians . . . really weird, especially when I was in college. One guy named Samuel (he would never let you call him Sam) was a fantastic tennis player. Because he thought tennis was a little unspiritual, you would have to coax him into playing. On the court he was a demon (he would never let you call him that, either!): smashing backhands; looping high, precise lobs; demolishing the ball with an overhead slam.

Instead of swearing, Samuel reserved a nice Christian-sounding word to shout just before creaming the ball. About every fourth serve, his back would arch more steeply than usual, he would toss the ball higher, and his feet would leave the ground. Just before his arm whipped forward to whack the ball, he'd grunt loudly, "'Lujah!"

I still shudder when I think of that word "'Lujah." Maybe Samuel meant it as an expression of his faith in God. But to me it was a final warning to dodge a missile that would come screaming over the net and kick up into my face. Though Samuel was pretty weird, he earned respect in almost any crowd by his inspired tennis playing.

Brian was the opposite—the butt of everyone's jokes. His 130 pounds were stretched along a 6'4" frame; and, maybe because he didn't have enough strength to hold himself up, he walked with a permanent forward bend, as if he had carried a heavy backpack during all his growing years. Brian talked shyly and softly, and his face was so pale and fragile that you couldn't help mentally picturing him as a ghost.

To compound matters, Brian had the peculiar habit of walking around on his toes, backward, memorizing Bible verses. That's the truth. Every night he would dress in a white sweatsuit, jog a loping mile, then cool off by walking in circles under a streetlight, *backward*. It was an eerie scene: Brian's forward-tilting body jerking backward along the perimeter of the streetlight's glow, his head bowed, straining to see the verse he'd printed on a card, mumbling to himself.

I admit, not all the Christians I knew were as weird as Samuel and Brian. But those two were given a special level of respect among Christians—as if their "'Lujah"—shouting and backward-walking-verse-memorizing elevated them to a special class. At the Christian college I attended, most people thought them more "spiritual" than others. Knowing them, I kept asking myself, "Is this what God wants?"

All the Christians, however, from Debbie, the blonde knock-out, to George, the math expert, shared the same traits which at first seemed every bit as weird as Samuel and Brian's eccentricities.

There was prayer, for example. The Christians I knew distorted events to make everything look like an answer to prayer. If an uncle sent an extra twenty-five dollars for school bills, they would grin and shout and call a prayer meeting to thank God for it. While some people on campus were sleeping off the night's activities, the super-Christians would sneak out of their rooms at 6:30 A.M. for a prayer meeting.

They seemed to take these "answers to prayer" as final proof that God was out there listening to them. I could always find some other explanation. "Maybe that uncle sent *all* his nephews twenty-five dollars this month," I would say. "Some of the nephews aren't

Christians. Was yours the only gift that answered a prayer?" They never discussed the frequent times God ignored their specific requests. Prayer, to me, was a foolish activity. Of what use was talking aloud to the walls?

But the super-Christians' earnestness dumbfounded me. Partly out of curiosity and partly out of a malicious desire to destroy their illusions, I started hanging around them, even acting "Christian." I made up some story about how I had gotten "saved" as a teenager, embellished it with dramatic details, and told it at one of the Christian sharing meetings. The response was unbelievable. Most of the girls were in tears. Everyone hugged me, said "Praise God!" and had a special prayer meeting of gratitude.

I began attending the prayer meetings—even the early morning eyepoppers—and imitated whatever the best Christians did. I learned the key to acceptance was a ritual called "giving your testimony" in which your voice took on a soft, sincere tone and you told of some way the Lord had blessed you or "spoken to you." I found after a few weeks that I was one of the best testimony-givers of the bunch. I could often bring the group to prayers of thanksgiving, or beckon tears from their hungry, searching eyes.

Meanwhile, I would race back to my dorm after these sessions and tell my real friends how thoroughly I was hoodwinking all the Christians.

"Sometimes Christianity just seems like a science, a state of mind, or a way of thinking. Is God really there, or did someone make it all up?"

In my mind, I had devastated their faith. I was a naturalist, and I believed there was no God. The only world existing was the world I lived in: Rocks, trees, and air. There were no "spiritual beings." Obviously their faith comprised spiritual jargon, a warm feeling of

closeness, and a guilt trip all thrown together. Though an avowed
unbeliever, I could pass for a veritable saint just by following the
prescribed formula. Theirs was no different from any other
misguided religion. How could God be real if all Christian
experience could be duplicated by someone who did not believe in
him?

The Plot Thickens

A strange thing happened about a year after this experiment. It
would have been humiliating and embarrassing had it not been so
overwhelmingly delightful. I became a Christian. God met me in an
amazing, undeniable way, at a time when I wasn't even looking for
him—in fact, while I was hotly denying him. I experienced a true
Christian conversion. During a routine (required) prayer meeting
with friends, God made contact with me. He showed me his love
and forgiveness, and I was born again.

Though I had spent my energy to that point trying to poke holes
in the Christian faith and to sniff out inconsistencies in Christians,
when God finally met me the change was so profound that I have
never doubted it since.

How could I describe this experience to my skeptical friends
whom I had succeeded in pushing toward agnosticism? How do you
describe a world of color to someone born color-blind? I found
myself mumbling the same imprecise phrases, like "God completely
transformed me" or "God has changed my whole way of thinking,
my sense of values" or "He's given me peace I have never known
before." Most of my friends looked at me with an unknowing,
confused, even *betrayed* look. I knew what they were thinking: "It's
finally gotten to the poor fellow. After months of hanging around
those super-Christians, imitating them, he's cracked. He's loony."

Frustrated, I tried to think of ways to persuade my friends that I
had not gone loony, but rather had found a deeper reality. I knew
they wouldn't be attracted to the Christians I knew—I had mocked
them too successfully. The idea of miracles came to me. Could I find

some absolutely unexplainable miracle? Surely that would prove God's reality.

Why wasn't God more obvious? I wanted him to conduct well-orchestrated, televised miracles so that I could invite my skeptical friends to see an act of God they could never deny. The problem, as I saw it, was that the Christian acts—praying, loving each other, sharing faith with others, worshiping—just weren't *supernatural* enough to convince anyone that Christianity is true. *What we really need, I thought, is a giant, world-wide awesome display of God's power.* Naturalism would topple to the ground.

Even as I thought that, I realized it wouldn't work. The Bible records scores of instances when God really shocked the world. The ten plagues of Egypt, for example. Cecil B. DeMille spent millions to imitate them, and his film sequences still look phony. What of the resurrection of Jesus? More than five hundred people attested that he had come back from the dead, but most people refused to believe them. God himself walked on earth for thirty-three years, teaching and performing astounding miracles. Yet, of those who heard him, only a minority believed.

Miracles—the wide open, fireworks, supernatural sort—will always be an exception. Oh, I believe they occur. Many of my friends tell me of some miraculous healing, or a dramatic change God worked in a drug addict. But those miracles which suspend the laws of nature for an instant—I must admit I have never seen one personally.

I don't need miracles to believe; God has lovingly proved himself to me. It only bothers me when I think about my skeptical friends. If God really did a miracle, right in front of their eyes, would they believe? I don't know.

Instead I am left with the simple, sometimes tedious Christian acts of praying, sharing, loving, serving. As I know too well from my early contacts with weird Christians, those acts fall short of convincing a skeptic. They can even be expertly duplicated as a joke or as a sociology experiment.

I never did come up with a good strategy for convincing skeptics. Some came to believe, some didn't. Some were attracted to

God by Christians' love; some fled to him when their world was crumbling. Many others, though, are far from God today.

TWO WORLDS

Today, even after all God has done for me, I have doubts. I will always believe he's real. But often my prayers seem like hollow, sleepy words that bounce off walls and rise no higher than my ceiling. Sometimes when I hear a fellow Christian describe an experience he has had with the Lord, it sounds no different from what you might hear at a Transcendental Meditation meeting or in an encounter group. It is still sometimes hard for me to believe— *really* believe—that there is another part of the world out there. I am never completely rid of naturalism, because the only world I *see* everyday is the natural one. How do I keep believing in an invisible world?

There is an evident world around me comprised of trees and rocks and people and cars and buildings. Everyone believes in that one. But there is an equally real world of angels and spirits and God and heaven and hell. If only I could see that other world, just once, perhaps that would solve all my doubts.

"I feel my friends and family members have been manipulated into living a Christian charade. I'm not going to be sucked in."

When these doubts surface, I think back to some of Jesus' teaching about the two worlds. One incident (in Luke 10) especially pulled the two worlds together. Jesus sent out seventy of his faithful followers to the towns and villages he planned to visit later. He warned them sternly that they might be mocked or even persecuted for representing him. "You are like lambs among wolves," he said.

The seventy disciples trudged away in the dust, certainly expecting the worst after Jesus' pessimistic warnings. But they returned exuberant. People had accepted them. Towns were eagerly awaiting the visit of Jesus. They had healed sick people. "Even the demons submit to us in your name, " they breathlessly reported.

Jesus, who had been waiting for their return, gave a unique summary of what had happened. He said, "I saw Satan fall like lightning from heaven!" Jesus brought the two worlds together. The world of the disciples had been one of walking over hot sand, preaching to mixed crowds, knocking on doors, asking to see the sick, announcing the coming of Jesus. All their actions took place in the visible world which you can touch, smell, and see. But Jesus, with supernatural insight, saw that those actions in the visible world were having a phenomenal impact on the invisible world. While disciples were grinding out spiritual victories in the visible world, Satan was falling to their onslaught in the invisible world.

In Luke 12, Jesus gave some more clues to the effect that what happens here in the visible world affects the other world. He said that whatever we whisper in the inner rooms, thinking we are alone and safe, will one day be broadcast from the housetops for all to hear. No act, even whispering, is going unnoticed in the world. Each is recording its mark in the invisible world.

Jesus said that when a sinner repents, the angels in heaven rejoice. Today you can watch a sinner repent. Turn on a Billy Graham crusade sometime and you can see, live and in color, many sinners repenting. The camera zooms in on a middle-aged businessman, head lowered, threading his way down the stadium seats to talk to a counselor. It moves to a young girl in Levis, quietly sobbing in a corner as a friend explains the Bible to her. According to what Jesus said, while those visible acts are taking place, some tremendous invisible acts are also occurring. The angels are throwing a celebration in heaven. The two worlds are working as one.

The man Jesus was, of course, the ultimate example of the two worlds working as one. He was a man with sweat glands, hair, fingernails, lips, and all the characteristics that define humans. Yet inside that body God lived.

All of us who are Christians believe in the invisible world; we merely forget about it. We get consumed by our world of arguments, relationships, jobs, and school—even the "religious" world of church and prayer meetings. Perhaps if Jesus were standing in the flesh beside us murmuring phrases like "I saw Satan fall" whenever God used us for some good, we would remember better.

The world we live in is not an "either/or" world. The actions I do as a Christian—praying, worshiping, loving—are not exclusively supernatural or natural. They are both, working at the same time.

Seeing the Invisible

As reminders of the supernatural world we are given God's Spirit, who permanently dwells within us. We are given the good counsel of the Bible and of fellow Christians, who affirm that, yes, there is another world, and God is alive and cares about us.

Besides all these specifically Christian reminders, there are many proofs of God in the world which can be detected by everyone. Do you wish to see an expression of God's power? Get up early to watch a sunrise. Visit California beaches during whale migration season and watch the great beasts frolic and sputter.

Do you question whether man is immortal? Consider your own reaction when you pass a dead cat or skunk or opossum on the road. You may feel a twinge of regret or sadness, especially if you love animals; but it is not at all the reaction you would feel if you passed a human body sprawled next to the pavement. You would gasp and screech to a halt. The memory would burn into your mind. You would never forget the scene. What is the difference? Both corpses are made of sinew, blood, bone, and organs. The difference is nothing visible; it is the fact that the person is immortal, made in God's image.

Sometimes I remember the invisible world clearly. I can sense its existence so strongly that it seems more real than the visible world. The quality of *faith* lets me believe—the quality that the book of Hebrews defines as "being sure of what we hope for and certain of what we do not see" (11:1). At those moments (I remember how I felt after my conversion) I wonder how anyone could doubt. Other times—often when I'm tired and irritable, and have just fought with someone—I can barely remember the invisible world. Those moments, too, are evidence of the great spiritual struggle going on behind the curtain, accompanying every moment of my life.

"There is no neutral ground in the universe," said C. S. Lewis. "Every inch, every split second, is claimed by God and counterclaimed by Satan."

I am strong enough to believe that on my own sometimes. I feel very much a part of a battle. But at other times I forget and must be pressed back to God, to his Word, to the helpless dependence on him and his followers here on earth. They remind me of the invisible world and my role in it. Satan does not give up his ground easily.

MICHAEL SILUK

Fact #12

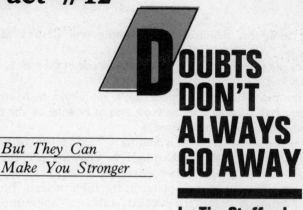

DOUBTS DON'T ALWAYS GO AWAY

But They Can
Make You Stronger

by Tim Stafford

My doubts about God come most often in crowds. I stand still and watch streams of people flow by me. Each person is intent on his own direction and his own thoughts. Each, I think, knows and cares nothing about my belief that there is a God who cares. I feel lonely and insignificant, numbed by the democracy of unbelief. Who am I to say that my reasoning makes more sense than theirs? They look so solid and sure in their business: How could I ever convince them of a God who loves them? They aren't even interested. I wonder if it is I who am crazy.

Does it make you uncomfortable to know that I, who should be a sturdy, reliable believer, have doubts? That there have been nights when I literally screamed at God, pleading for some signal that he is real? There was a time when I felt threatened if a Christian told me of his own deep questions. If others thought of deserting the ship, was I only kidding myself to keep on believing? Besides, I thought doubts were the worst danger to a Christian.

I do not think so now. Doubts are serious. Sometimes they lead to rejection of God. But more often, I think, if confronted honestly, they can lead to a stronger faith.

Other things worry me more.

It worries me when someone is knowingly disobeying God and

rationalizing away his disobedience. Nothing will destroy faith sooner.

It worries me when someone pastes on a facade of vibrant faith, while doubts and loneliness lurk behind.

It worries me when a Christian can't get along with other Christians, but has a list as long as your arm of how he or she has been cheated, abused, or mistreated.

It worries me when someone is finding a "new, more mature" faith that finds unnecessary such things as knowing the Bible, praying and worshiping with other Christians.

But doubts? They have their place, in the Bible at least. From the flaming questions of Job to the puzzled, stubborn "Show me" of Thomas, doubts are handled frankly. Doubters are brave enough to ask questions; in fact, it is the pious people who seem to anger God more by knowing all the answers and quickly shutting-up questioners.

When you are doubting God's existence, it may help to figure out just what is in doubt. Analyze your problem before you look for a solution. But do seek answers. The walls of Christian faith are not so thin that you will break holes in them by pushing too hard. If you ask honestly, you will find answers—though not always the answers you would have liked. "Seek and you will find," Jesus promised. "Knock and the door will be opened to you" (Matthew 7:7). That was a promise to his disciples. They had chosen to follow him. Having done so, they heard the promise from Jesus himself, who founded the earth, that they would not remain puzzled forever, so long as they were willing to seek and ask.

THREE KINDS OF DOUBTS

Lonely doubts, I think, are the most common. I talked recently with a friend who had been going through a difficult time doubting whether God exists or cares at all. But recently her thinking changed. "I realized," she said, "that I was really lonely. I knew all these people, but none of them really knew me. So I was angry with

God, yelling at him that I didn't have any friends. That was the real source of my doubts."

It is hard to believe in God's love when there are no people around who love you. It takes unusual strength to live through such a period without severe doubts. We are meant to experience God's love through people, as well as through God himself.

But if you are lonely, make sure that is the focus of your doubts. Do not go on a philosophical tangent about those suffering in India. Speak to God about the reality of human friendship, and ask him to begin to show you how to make one good friend. Ask him, too, to show some purpose in your loneliness, some way you should grow through it. It won't happen overnight, but with a sense of direction your doubts about God will fade. He will become your ally, rather than your antagonist, in healing loneliness.

Crisis doubts are often the most intense. Someone you love dies. Perhaps your best friend rejects you. Finals at school destroy you. Often during a crisis, you are very tired without even knowing it. The mental strain makes you need far more rest, and you often get no physical exercise. The pressure will not let up, and you are constantly nervous.

"I never used to feel lonely because I always felt God was with me. I even studied the Bible in study hall at school. But lately my loneliness has returned, unless I am with friends. I am lonely around my family and sometimes even when I talk to God. He isn't as much of a companion anymore."

In *God and Man at Yale*, William F. Buckley said that whenever he had doubts about God he would lie down until he got over them. It is not so bad a prescription. Often doubts, and particularly crisis doubts, are a response to powerful feelings of sadness fueled by fatigue. They will pass. Of course, crises can and should start questions that have lasting implications. But don't delude yourself by thinking that you can settle the meaning of the universe in one evening when you are low on sleep. You are not in any shape to do that. Recognize that you are in a crisis, ask your questions, but store them until later. Sleep if you can. Look to a friend for comfort. Often all it takes is a chance to express your doubts, and they fly away. If they do not, don't make any great decisions. Wait to resolve your questions later when you are rested.

Intellectual doubts are actually, I believe, least common of all. The reason is that very few of us are intellectuals. But many of us wish we were, and it is hard for us to admit that we cannot figure out all the answers for ourselves. So we phrase many of our doubts as intellectual questions, partly to keep at a distance our own loneliness and inadequacy.

There are, however, really good questions to be asked about the reality of Jesus Christ. If God is good, why is he willing to send some people to hell? How can we say that Christianity is better than Hinduism? Why do people suffer? If offering our lives to God really makes us new creatures, how come Christians often seem no better than anyone else? How can we put trust in a book as unscientific as the Bible? There are many more.

I am not going to try to answer those questions here, though I believe there are good answers. We may not find final, once-for-all answers to questions. But we will find answers that have satisfied men and women a great deal smarter and more learned than we. (A good starting place might be the writings of C. S. Lewis, particularly *Mere Christianity* and *The Problem of Pain*.)

The saddest thing to me is that those who ask intellectual questions often decide the answers—and their whole life—on the basis of a few vague ideas floating around in their heads, or something a professor in college said with assurance, or on information in a couple of once-over-lightly textbooks. There is better information in any library or bookstore and, I would hope, in any pastor's office.

If you are having intellectual doubts, follow them honestly to the end. Ask questions of people who are likely to have answers, and ask a number of people—don't settle for one or two. Ask for reading material. It may take some time, but since you are trying to decide whether your life as a Christian has meaning, isn't the question worth some serious study? If it is not—if you are content with the rummage sale of information in your brain already—then I doubt whether you are really being honest in your questions. If you give up your faith, you have cheated yourself. If you maintain your faith, you have cheated yourself too: These questions may come up again, or your faith may become superficial if you are afraid to confront difficult doubts and listen honestly to questions non-Christians are asking.

If you ask honestly and are willing to ask God for help, I think you will find answers that satisfy. That is what has happened to me time and time again.

The Ultimate Answer

My doubt is more emotional than intellectual; I know that because it comes when I am tired. Still, it is real. I get weary of being different. Sometimes I would like to drop back into thinking what everyone else thinks. Instead of worrying about other people, instead of reading the Bible and praying and going to church, I would like just to think and do what *I* feel like. Being a Christian seems to be a tiresome ritual I'm caught in.

So what happens when I have these doubts? One thing that needs to happen, of course, is sleep. But there is more than that. My questions are not bad ones. What *is* the point of all these rituals we go through? Why *do* Christians act and think in such an odd way? I am forced back to the foundation of my faith. It comes down to this: if it were not for Jesus, I don't think I would be a Christian.

Now, isn't that an absurd sentence? If it weren't for Jesus, there would be *no* Christians. There would be no Christianity. But, obvious as the point is, it needs to be made. Sometimes I think our version of Christianity could cruise along without Jesus. If someone somehow proved Jesus never lived or never came back to life, we might get along just as well. We get rosy feelings from singing songs together. We make good friends through church or Christian groups. We have a point of view for looking at the world, and that breeds security. We talk about Jesus, but that seems to be a coded language for our good feelings. It doesn't attach to any real person— a person as definite as, say, my father. Could we substitute any other name for "Jesus" and, once we got comfortable with it, do just as well? Would "Buddha" do?

Suppose that someone lives Christianity just that way—strictly as a way of life, without really thinking of it as a relationship with Jesus, a real, living Person. I suspect the person might keep to the pattern all his life, enjoying being a Christian in the same way people enjoy being Republicans. Over the years he would grow to understand the system better—he would know how to argue over crucial points, where to find things in the Bible, and have theories about how a church should run. But he would probably not grow kinder or more compassionate or closer to the source of life. He might spend his life confusing the good feelings he gets from praying in a group of friends with the reality of God. He might never know he had missed anything.

I think most people start with Christianity and only gradually grow to know Christ. We are attracted by a group of people, a way of life, a leader or friend we trust.

That is my experience. I grew up in a fine Christian family. I have known some wonderful Christian leaders. I have been in some great churches, some exciting fellowships where things were really happening. But as good as all that is, it is not enough. You have to go beyond. Though some of the Christianity I have been around has been very good, long dry spells still came when my faith didn't mean much to me, or when I was without much support from other Christians.

But what I cannot get around, even when I'm unhappy, is the

man known as Jesus. He is amazing. The more I learn about him, the more astonished I become. He is the ultimate answer to my doubts.

The Only Truly Free Man

You have to read about him. In fact, there isn't any other completely reliable way to learn about him. Four pamphlets give reasonably detailed accounts of his life on earth, when his character took on a visible focus. It is no accident that the New Testament begins with them: Matthew, Mark, Luke, and John. They are basic.

What do I find in these four accounts of Jesus? I find layer after layer of meaning; simplicity I can understand the first time I read it; and richness the greatest of minds never exhausts. I find a convincing portrait of the only Man I would think it is worth dying to follow.

It is not just what he said. It is not just his ability to do amazing things. It is not just the way he loved people. It is not just his character under stress. It is not just his astonishing relationship with God. Incredibly, he combined all those things. He is unique; there is nothing and no one like him.

I could talk about many aspects of Jesus and why he appeals to me. But I will limit myself to telling you just one thing that always amazes me about him. Jesus is the only completely free Man I have ever encountered.

I want so much to be free. I don't want to be imprisoned by anything. I want to soar as wildly as a hawk playing in the wind. In Jesus I see a model for what I want to become.

By "free" I do not mean free from all constriction or responsibility. People who have that kind of freedom are often tragically enslaved. Rock stars, with all the money and time to do what they like, sometimes commit suicide or strangle slowly on drugs. Some of the freest people seem to be those under intense pressure, like Aleksandr Solzhenitsyn or the apostle Paul in prison.

The freedom I am interested in starts inside. I figure we will always have some limits imposed from the outside. I am more concerned about the limits we have inside. A really free person is able to laugh when others are bitter; he can be kind when others hate; he can be in a room full of gossip and not participate; he can be himself no matter what pressures are on him.

Jesus was free. Crowds adored him, but he did not live to please them. Hundreds of sick people came to him to be healed, but he did not let that pressure keep him from priorities like spending time in prayer. The religious establishment criticized him, but he did not let that intimidate him, nor did he let it push him into becoming a stereotyped rebel. His best friends had ideas about how he should act and the kind of future he should expect, but he would not be influenced.

Jesus' freedom flowed from his identity as God's Son. He kept in contact; he remembered who he was in relation to God. The pressures could not mold him, because God did not change in his love and his promise to keep him together. Even death could not take away who he was—and is.

For me, his most amazing display of freedom was in front of a rigged court that was obviously bent on murdering him. These were the religious people; they were also everything he had stood against. Now, in the ultimate display of perverted piousness, they had him in their power. They didn't even have the courage to kill him outright: They had to try him on phony charges.

If you can imagine being accused of bribery in front of the Senate by the best-known cheat in Congress, you might have a hint of the mix of fury and fear natural to anyone in that situation.

Most of us have enough guilt stored up to feel we deserve punishment of some kind. When my car breaks down, I glumly, fatalistically accept it as something I deserve. But Jesus had done *nothing* wrong, not one thing in his whole life. He had never felt guilt.

So wouldn't you expect Jesus angrily to defend himself? Or to try to talk his way out of death? Or to beg?

He did not. At his trial he was repeatedly asked if he believed himself to be the Messiah, the Son of God. He was challenged to defend himself. He never did.

Why? In Luke 22:67–68 Jesus says why: "If I tell you, you will not believe me, and if I asked you, you would not answer." Even under threat of a grossly unfair, torturous death, Jesus remembered who he was. He knew they had the roles reversed. He was the judge of the world, and they were the ones who needed to defend themselves. They could play at mock trials, but he wasn't going to be caught in their game.

That was not arrogance. It was reality. The unreality was the trial, which tried to overrule the position God had given Jesus. He went to his death a perfectly free man. Even on the cross, in horrible pain, he was himself. What did he do in those last, agonizing hours while he felt his body dying? He forgave a thief. He initiated a family relationship between his mother and John. He committed his life to God.

I can't get over that. When I read what happened I am astonished. I know that I have found contact with Someone worth following. I conquer my doubts. Not only that, I give thanks for my doubts, for they have led me closer to Jesus himself.

Your doubts can often lead to a deeper understanding of God, for his answers will seldom be just the kind you were expecting. If your beliefs are shallow, then they will have to be dredged deeper. If the skeleton of your faith has grown crooked, bones may have to be broken before they can be reset. It will hurt. But don't be afraid: Broken bones set stronger.

Epilogue

STRATEGY FOR PEOPLE WITH QUESTIONS

by Verne Becker

By now you've probably figured out that clear-cut answers to your doubts will not come easily—and possibly not at all. But you will indeed find some answers—though they may catch you by surprise. And you will learn and grow as you pursue your doubts.

In this final chapter I've tried to assemble some of the best advice I've received from people I've shared my doubts with. Consider the following tips, not as a do-this-and-your-doubts-will-vanish formula, but rather as a list of suggestions that you can follow or reflect on as you deal with your doubts and questions. I trust that it will help you as it did me.

1. *Be honest with yourself.* Are your doubts real, or are you trying to avoid facing up to something you already know is true?

2. *Give yourself the freedom to doubt.* Dismiss all notions that doubting is sinful or inappropriate. Doubt does not equal unbelief. If you are a true doubter, remind yourself that you are a special person, one who won't settle for a simplistic view of life. Allowing yourself to search for answers to your doubts will lead you down the path of spiritual growth rather than spiritual stagnation.

Remember you're in good company. Throughout the Bible people doubted. Read through the Psalms or examine the lives of biblical characters such as Job, David, Solomon (particularly in Ecclesiastes), John the Baptist, Thomas, and others to see how doubts are expressed and answered.

Virtually everyone experiences doubts at some time in life, though some may doubt more than others. Jay Kesler has referred to a handy formula called the 90/10 rule: Examine your feelings, and assume 90 percent of the world feels the same way. If you doubt, probably most of the people around you do, too.

Even atheists and agnostics doubt their "faith."

3. *Get the facts straight.* Just what is causing you to doubt? Can you pinpoint the exact cause? Is it an inexplicable *event*, such as death, divorce, illness, or some other tragedy? Is it *new information*, such as something a teacher said about evolution, or a puzzling statement you read in a book? Or is it a *person*—someone in your youth group who professes faith in God but parties all the time? A Christian friend you trusted who failed you? The better handle you can get on the cause of your doubt, the better your chance of finding answers.

4. *Separate truth from behavior.* Many nonbelievers say their biggest hang-up with Christianity is Christians. They see Christian friends at school who are snobs, or a Christian man who cheats on his wife, or a manipulative TV preacher milking viewers for money, and they say, "If this is what being a Christian is like, I don't want any part of it." They have a point: Christians who do stupid things in God's name don't represent him very well to the rest of the world. But does that mean that the gospel is untrue?

If you're working on a geometry problem and incorrectly apply the Pythagorean Theorem, does that mean the theorem is false? Or is it rather that you began with something true and misused it? The same goes for Christianity: Whether it's true doesn't depend on the behavior of its followers.

5. *Take your biological/emotional temperature.* Do your doubts parallel mood swings brought on by loneliness, fatigue, monthly cycles, or frantic schedules? Listen to your moods and to your body.

Go to bed. Eat less sugar. Get involved in a prayer or Bible study group. Reduce your commitments if necessary. Or maybe you simply need to wait it out and see if your doubts pass.

6. *Explore how your doubts about God relate to your personal worldview.* For instance, if as a child you had a bad relationship to your father, you may find it difficult, even abhorrent, to think of God as your heavenly Father. Try to identify things in your family relationships that have affected your outlook on life and your ways of thinking and feeling. A good conversation with your grandparents, for instance, can yield plenty of insight into your parents'—and therefore your own—worldview.

7. *Confront your doubts directly.* Don't let them paralyze you. Instead, wrestle with them and search for answers. Read the Bible; read other books; talk to your pastor or youth director; share your questions with your family and friends.

8. *Express your doubts to God.* Don't be afraid to talk directly to God about your questions. He is bigger than all our doubts—he can handle them. And he won't punish you for being honest with him. God is not a force, but a Person; don't hesitate to approach him as a person. And realize that he cares for *you* personally.

9. *Give yourself time to get to know God better.* Spend time alone with him, reading the Bible, praying, worshiping, listening as well as talking. Meet him in different settings—in the woods, in the mountains, in your room, in a cathedral, while you jog. Visit several different kinds of churches for a fresh perspective. If you attend a Baptist or independent church, visit a more formal, liturgical service

> "I try to be patient. I know God is helping me to grow in every aspect of my life. I know I will always have doubts, but God is using these to teach me more."

at a Lutheran or Episcopal church (or vice-versa). Churches and denominations emphasize different things. For example, Presbyterian and Reformed churches tend to focus on the sovereign rule of God over the world. Pentecostal and charismatic assemblies give more attention to spiritual gifts, healing, and miracles. Perhaps a change of church scenery will broaden your outlook and help resolve some of your doubts.

10. *Listen for God's voice in a variety of places.* We tend to underestimate God's ability to speak to us. We often assume God does little more than occasionally make a sick friend well or help us find a parking place. But suppose the problem is not with him, but with us? Actually, God is speaking to us all the time, in many different ways; we just aren't hearing him. Why? Because we haven't trained ourselves to tune in to his voice. (By *voice* I don't mean audible sound as much as a sense of God's presence in a situation.)

What are some ways God can speak to us? The Bible, of course, is God's clearest and most authoritative statement to humanity. But he can speak in other ways, too: through prayer, through circumstances, through feelings, through dreams, through miracles, through healing, through music, through other people, in worship, in nature. Some of these channels may give you fuzzier reception than others, but if you listen carefully, God's voice will come through.

The messages God sends, however, may not be what you expect or want. God tends not to say things like "Take the job" or "Marry Susan"; more often he will say "I'm here with you," "I love you," "Trust me," or "I'll take care of you." He's less interested in the decisions we make than in our awareness that he's present and involved in our lives.

(A footnote: God never contradicts himself. We can test the validity of a message we think is from God by comparing it to the clear messages of Scripture. If the message opposes biblical teaching, we should reject it.)

Many doubt God because they have never encountered him personally—that is, because they haven't tuned in to his voice. God has been knocking at their door for years, perhaps, but they haven't answered it. Is God speaking to you in some way? Will you listen? Just knowing he is there may make all the difference in living with your doubts.

11. *Focus on Jesus Christ.* Christianity would ultimately be meaningless without Christ. His life, his teachings, and his victory over sin and death are the foundation upon which faith is built. Read the four Gospels carefully, allowing yourself to experience the feelings those around him must have felt, and applying his teaching to the daily events and relationships in your life. Jesus Christ has a way of getting through to people, penetrating hard shells of skepticism or resistance and meeting them face to face.

12. *Relax in what you already know.* Remember how many of the important questions in life God *does* answer. The Bible contains everything you need to know to meet God personally, to live the kind of life that will make a difference in the world, and to travel through death into eternal glory with God. Scripture also devotes space (Job, the Psalms, Ecclesiastes, Romans 9–11, and other places) to wrestling with some of the unanswerable questions you may be asking. But this material represents a fairly small portion of the Bible. Is it possible that this small proportion indicates how important God thinks it is for us to have these answers? If he had wanted us to have these answers while sojourning on earth, wouldn't he have given them to us?

13. *Remember that all truth is God's truth.* It's one thing to say the Bible contains everything *we need* to know, and quite another to say it contains everything *there is* to know. Sometimes we fall into the trap of assuming there are two kinds of truth—spiritual and secular. We erroneously think that spiritual truth, basically the Bible, is the only truth that matters. Secular truth, which includes everything from how to unclog a drain to medical science to psychotherapy to quarks, is somehow "less true" or unimportant because it doesn't refer directly to God or because non-Christians promote it.

This schizophrenic view of truth ignores the fact that God created everything in the world, and that ultimately all truth has its source in God. So long as we do not contradict the teaching of Scripture, we are free to explore, to discover truth—God's truth—wherever it may be found.

14. *Expect to learn and grow from the searching process itself.* Just as Jacob wrestled with God and emerged a changed person (Genesis 32:22–32), so you can expect to change and grow as you wrestle with your doubts. As you struggle, and as you find some answers, you may discover that the answers don't mean nearly as much to you as the process of searching for them. You may even end up like many people who have said, "I don't care what the answer is anymore, but I know God is there for me and that's all that matters."

15. *Realize that life isn't so simple.* The kind of hard questions you are asking rarely have black-and-white, yes-or-no answers. Though God does not contradict himself, the world seems to overflow with contradictions. Terrorist groups blow innocent people to bits. Thousands starve to death in Ethiopia while Americans get fatter each day. Devout religious leaders perform barbaric acts in the name of their god.

How can these things be reconciled with a loving, all-powerful God who's in control of the world? The simple answer is that there is no simple answer. We cannot explain (in other than very general terms) why things happen as they do. We are finite human beings who cannot even pretend to understand the mysteries of an infinite God.

There comes a point when we must say, "I don't know." Many Christians are afraid to say those three words. Instead, they come up with simplistic answers and phrases, feeling that they must somehow cover up for God's inadequacies. It certainly hurts to say, "I don't know." But it may be the most honest thing we can tell people—or ourselves.

16. *Let God be God.* Not all the questions we ask *have* answers this side of heaven. But then, isn't that the way it should be? If God is the Creator and we are his creations, doesn't it make sense for him to know more than we do? We can question him and cry out to him, but we can never understand him completely. Sometimes we need to acknowledge and accept God's "god-ness."

"Oh, what a wonderful God we have!" writes the apostle Paul in Romans 11:33–36. "Oh, the depth of the riches of the wisdom and knowledge of God! How unsearchable his judgments, and his paths beyond tracing out! 'Who has known the mind of the Lord? Or who has been his counselor?' 'Who has ever given to God, that God should repay him?' For from him and through him and to him are all things. To him be the glory forever! Amen."